How to
Write
a Love
Letter

How to Write a Love Letter

Putting What's in Your Heart on Paper

BARRIE DOLNICK
and DONALD BAACK

Harmony Books
New York

To future generations:
May they carry on this written
tradition of love.

Published by Harmony Books, New York, New York. Member of the Crown Publishing Group.

Random House, Inc.
New York, Toronto, London, Sydney, Auckland
www.randomhouse.com

HARMONY BOOKS is a registered trademark and the Harmony Books colophon is a trademark of Random House, Inc.

Printed in the United States of America

Design by Donna Sinisgalli

Library of Congress Cataloging-in-Publication Data
Dolnick, Barrie.
How to write a love letter: putting what's in your heart on paper / Barrie Dolnick and Donald Baack.
1. Love letters.   I. Baack, Donald.   II. Title.
HQ801.3.D65   2000
306.7 — dc21   00-056741

ISBN 0-609-60727-8

10 9 8 7 6 5 4 3 2 1

First Edition

Acknowledgments

Many people have contributed their ideas, support, stories, and letters of love to this project.

Emma Sweeney, my agent and friend, who shared not only her wisdom and assistance but also the precious words of her father's last letter; Shaye Areheart, whose thought, warm heart, and energy pulled this collaboration together. My friends who pointed out love in every corner of the world: Ann, Cheryl, Friedel, Halo, Jen, Jennie, Julia, Liz, Mary Lou, Sheila, and Susan. My sisters, who possess a sweet and biting wit that picks me up when I'm down. My mom, whose belief in my ability to write and to love kept me going.

Special thanks to Don Baack, a generous man with big ideas, an abundance of love in his life, and commitment to his passion for writing.

And, of course, to my Elisabeth, who I hope will receive many beautifully written love letters in her life. And to Gero, my love and inspiration, for putting up with a shortage of our own love letters for a while.

— B . D .

I would like to thank Peter Rubie for overseeing my interests in this project. Also, Lisa Kaufman has been a wonderful help to me in my publishing efforts. My parents, Rev. Edward and Jean Baack, are wonderful role models of the true and genuine meaning of love, to each other as spouses, and to me as part of a terrific family. My loving wife, Pam, is the inspiration for all that I do, from writing to simply waking up in the morning. She has turned my life into an adventure, and a joy. Finally, I wish to thank Barrie. It has been a delight collaborating with her on this book.

— D . B .

Contents

Memory will slip;
a letter will keep.

—WELSH PROVERB

Introduction

I remember the first note of affection I received in high school. I remember the clammy anticipation of opening it up, the eagerness to read it but still savor every word. I knew the writer. I had a crush on this guy. He chatted lightly to me in his note, but he said one thing that thrilled me. It wasn't sexy, or lusty (thank goodness). He simply said that he couldn't stop thinking about me. I read and reread that letter until it was limp like a tissue. I'd never felt that way before. I'm so grateful that he took the time and gathered up his courage to write that down.

—SANDY, 54, TOLEDO, OHIO

No one can resist a love letter. Not a cool teenager, not a grumpy old geezer — not the most logical, tough-minded, callous-hearted individual around. There is not one heart on this planet that won't melt under the influence of a love letter. When someone takes the time to tell you how much you mean and takes the time to write it down — well, let's just agree it's very touching.

A love letter is an amazing thing: a letter written to you by someone you care about, with words that reveal deliberate thought, passion, and intention. Receiving a love letter and the thrill of reading it can spark one of those moments in your life that lingers forever in your memory, a warm secret.

We wanted to write this book to help more people create those remarkable touchstones and to convey messages that somehow feel more real and more powerful on paper, and even on your E-mail. We know it's hard to do. We know it's hard to get it right. We know that somehow, we all want to be great writers, capable of poignant, powerful words. But we're not all that gifted.

Here's our secret: you don't have to be that talented to write the best love letter you'd ever imagine. All you need is the object of your affection — a boyfriend, girlfriend, partner, spouse — or just an eye for the one you want (love letters can be great forms of flirtation).

We're here to help you with this. We—that is, Don Baack and I—are going to guide you through this infinitely imaginative process to find your best voice (on paper) to convey your best intentions in the most creative, compelling, and passionate way possible. If you're already thinking this isn't going to happen, think again.

With both the female point of view (that's me) and the male point of view (obviously, that's Don), we'll cover all those manifestations of love and like—whispers, sonnets, and epics—to find the best way to say what you want to say.

Why Bother?

Sure, love letters seem a little old-fashioned, but at the same time, they are so totally modern. Novels, plays, and poetry have been written solely around love letters. We all want to get one. We all want to have someone express his or her love for us so beautifully with words that we will hold onto those words, savor them, recall the feeling they evoke— maybe even carry them to our final days.

It's true.

Tender words; passionate murmurs; soft, delicate sentiments might seem out of your orbit. What about flirtations, apologies, or "I want to talk to you" messages? They can and should be love letters, too.

So few of us make use of our ability to write our feelings down. We're afraid that those words will mock us one day or that our offering will not be returned or, worse, will be scorned.

If you want to know how worthwhile a love letter can be, check out the Bible. Solomon couldn't stop talking about the love of his life. Whoever recorded this beautiful love poetry was pretty awestruck by the passion and considered it holy; the Song of Songs is a huge love letter right in the middle of the Old Testament, keeping these ancient flames alive for us to share.

Love letters are found throughout history. Recently, the British Library put on display what they think was the first valentine. Written in 1477, the valentine message is from Margery Brews of Norfolk to her fiancé, John Paston. In it she tells him that her mother has put pressure on her father to increase her dowry without success—while at the same time telling John that if he loves her, he'll marry her anyway.

Unto my right well-beloved Valentine John Paston, squire, be this bill delivered.

Right reverent and worshipful and my right well-beloved valentine. I recommend me unto you full heartedly, desiring to hear of your welfare, which I beseech Almighty God long for to preserve unto his pleasure and your heart's desire. And if it pleases you to hear of my welfare, I am not in good health of body nor of heart, nor shall I be till I hear from you.

For there knows no creature what pain that I endure.

And even on the pain of death I would reveal no more.

And my lady my mother hath laboured the matter to my father full diligently, but she can no more get than you already know of, for which God knoweth I am full sorry. But if you love me, as I trust verily that you do, you will not leave me therefore. For even if you had not half the livelihood that you have, for to do the greatest labour that any woman alive might, I would not forsake you. And if you command me to keep me true wherever I go, indeed I will do all my might you to love and never anyone else. And if my friends say that I do amiss, they shall not stop me from doing so. My heart me bids evermore to love you truly over all earthly things. And if they be never so angry, I trust it shall be better in time coming.

No more to you at this time, but the Holy Trinity have you in keeping. And I beseech you that this bill be not seen by any non earthly creature save only yourself.

And this letter was written at Topcroft with full heavy heart. 🌿

To us, her letter sounds studied and formal (even though this is a modernized version of her text!). I assure you this won't be the way you'll write.

You can borrow from history without sounding ancient. After all, so many great writers have written classics centered around their passions. Edmond Rostand wrote *Cyrano de Bergerac,* a novel about a man with a nose so grotesque he felt too ugly to be loved. You might remember this story from the Hollywood movie *Roxanne,* which starred Steve Martin and Daryl Hannah. In Rostand's love story, Cyrano hides behind a handsome man named Christian, to convey his messages of love. Cyrano eventually learns that his words, not the good looks of the other man, won Roxanne's affections.

> *"Unanimously, believe it, my heart cries out to you, and if kisses could be sent in writing, Love, you should read my letter with your lips . . ."*

There's a big lesson here: words are sexy. It is really cool when you realize that someone thinks about you in a way that makes him or her want to write—to put those special feelings into words.

Carefully considered thoughts, not flip, split-second retorts (like Instant Messages), are very, very potent.

Naturally, we won't all share Cyrano's poetic ramblings. After all, he is a fictional character living in seventeenth-century France. Today, we live in a vastly different reality.

Modern Romance and the Written Word

Today's romantic landscape is a minefield of potential pitfalls, including high expectations (we all want perfect love) and deep longings (the soulmate concept). Couple that with the media's obsession with physical perfection, sex, and sexuality, and your romantic legs can get a little wobbly. How can anyone live up to the larger-than-life Hollywood images of beauty, passion, and loving commitment? The pressure to live up to perfection and the fear of making a big mistake pretty much stymie modern written romance.

Does a love letter imply some kind of commitment or contract? After all, we live in a ferociously litigious society; can a letter be used against you?

What if you have a terrible breakup and your

letters are passed around for others to inspect and insult? Ouch.

Writing a love letter can seem terribly daunting: What if you feel as if you can't live up to what you write? What if you can't write as well as you can talk, or touch? Who has time to write a love letter, anyway? That's all a lot of baloney, but I've heard every one of those excuses from the fearful, timid, and lazy people who don't want to make the effort.

There may be nothing more important and honorable in your life than expressing your love (or like) for someone else. So don't pass up an opportunity to write a love letter.

1. No one expects you to be perfect (except maybe your parents).
2. Contracts can be oral, too—and there's no legal action if your feelings change.
3. Anyone who has the bad taste to display your intimate messages in public comes off worse than you do.
4. It's not that hard to write a love letter and you're going to learn a lot more about it here.

Ye Olden Times might have been more conducive to effusive, romantic love and the written word. It was even more stylish, to some extent, but there really is no lack of desire today, just (maybe) a lack of skill. It takes a courageous heart to commit itself to paper, but the intention is noble and, more often than not, the sentiment expressed becomes a precious, timeless gift.

Love-Letter Legacies

Love letters are keepsakes, a legacy. Your children, or at least your grandchildren, will be proud to find them and will enjoy reading them. The love letters kept in your family constitute an emotional archive, safely stored memories that won't yellow or fade, a key to what brought you together in the first place.

My Dear Elizabeth,

You know that this great war is not a thing I will tell you about. It is brutal and lonely and that is all I want to say.

But, if the Lord decides that I should be one of His soldiers I will have no choice but to do His bidding. If that day comes, this letter should be read aloud to our boys.

Harold, Joe Jr., Francis — they are the future of our love. And our love, my dearest E, started when you pretended not to notice me at church, when I was just a new face in a tiny town. Those bouncing curls of yours just wouldn't stay in their place and with you tugging at them every now and then—I knew I had to make you my wife one day. You are as pretty and stubborn as your curls.

Maybe it's not the most romantic story, but it's ours and it gives me a place to go when it's dark and cold and I miss you. If I don't come home, I want you to leave that story behind, though, and move on. You are a beautiful, lovely woman and I have three boys to show the world that you loved me once. You have too much love to be a silly widow for long, though. If some nice guy comes around and earns high marks with you, then you have my blessing to start a new life with him.

Don't let our boys tell you anything else, either. They'll try to, of course, because they're half made of me. But then, that gives me such comfort, too. You'll be loved and taken care of, no matter what.

So that is what is in my heart tonight. Be warm, take care of yourself, my lovely one, and know that I love you forever more.

Joseph

Creative Fun and Exploration

Love letters are not just sentimental or bare-hearted romantic musings. You can also use the written word for fun, flirtation, and conversation.

In writing love letters, you might even find out about yourself. You might not realize your talent for expression; maybe you're a poet, a lyricist—or a rapper (without the beat). Your creative vein may be flowing with gold, and working out how to articulate your emotions on paper is a large part of mining this gold.

You'll learn what brings you inspiration: books, music, nature, art, even the mundane acts of life like talking or walking or a simple sigh. Love letters are expressions of your romantic impulses. You could be inspired by the way your beloved looks at you in the morning or how he or she puts your child to bed. Inspiration is born out of moments when you're off guard and open to the love you feel. You could find your voice at three o'clock in the morning as easily as at three o'clock in the afternoon. Your message might be worthy of an independent film or as funny as an old Bugs Bunny cartoon. It's all about you, your personality, and your intention.

Writing allows you to express the more poetic sentiments that you may hesitate to say out loud.

Out loud: "You have such nice skin."
Written down: "Your skin looks like silk and is even softer. I love to look at it, to touch you with my eyes."

Sometimes you might want to say something but not know quite how. We've all come to rely on greeting cards to help us, but you can do more with them. Like "doctoring" a cake mix with chocolate chips to make it more homemade, you can add a few words to a card you buy to make it more personal, too. You can even buy a simple photograph, postcard, or blank card to help you visualize your message and add some flavor to your words. Be warned, though, you need to add your own words. Cards without a little personal oomph look too much like a convenience and can come off as phony.

I once used a card with a photograph of a man standing far away on a long, lonely highway to tell my husband how I felt about him going away for the first time since our wedding. I borrowed a quote from Wordsworth and added to it.

> *The silence that is in the starry sky,*
> *The sleep that is among the lonely hills,*
> *Is my company while you're away.*
> *I miss you already, my love.*

I wasn't prepared for how much it touched him. He called me that night after he'd found the card in his suitcase and I could hear the softness in his voice. Better still, he keeps it, so that he can look at it again and remember.

Once you see how easy it is to say what you feel, you'll enjoy experimenting with many ways to say it.

But Will You Do It? Can You Write?

You don't have to become the Romance Writer of the Year to pen a decent love letter. You don't even have to be romantic (right away). You can use letters just to talk, to get to know someone in a different way. It may well be best if you start out that way, with simple "practice" expressions, in order to get used to writing with this intimate purpose.

Love letters encourage written conversation. You might start with a simple expression of interest, but it can evolve into a little back-and-forth game and gradually grow into shared intimacy and trust. All on paper.

When my friend Steven drove a few people home from a party, he dropped off a girl he didn't know last. She was very nice but he felt weird asking for her phone number. All he had was her address.

☙ *Dear Harriet,*

It was nice to meet you at Todd's party. I'm only sorry I didn't have a chance to get to know you a little bit more. Would you be free next Saturday afternoon around three o'clock to get some ice cream at the Milky Way? I'll even spring for two scoops.

Yours truly,
Steven Ross
23 Beckerson Way ℘

☙ *Dear Steven,*

Thank you for your invitation. I'd love to join you on Saturday. I like chocolate and strawberry.

Best wishes,
Harriet
555-3210 ℘

Good old Steven initiated a lovely relationship with Harriet. That was back in 1953. They have three grown children and seven grandchildren today. Steven still remembers how much his hand shook when he mailed that letter—and how relieved he was to receive Harriet's response so quickly. His grandchildren never tire of that story, and Harriet still has her letter to prove it.

Sure, that was in the early fifties, when it was "hip to be square," but it's still cool to write it out.

Love letters can really be written anywhere—on a cocktail napkin, on a menu at the first restaurant you visit. You can use any kind of writing tool and any inspiration.

Don's List for Why Guys Should Write Love Letters

1. Women save love letters. (My wife did.)
2. Women love romantic things. (Note the popularity of romance novels and chick flicks.)
3. Lots of men want to say romantic things, and they don't know how. Being verbal can be clumsy, and writing gives you time to get it right.
4. Writing a love letter may help you discover or spell out your own feelings.
5. You may learn something about yourself. A guy who does lots of male-bonding crap is constantly taught to be insensitive and "masculine." That's why we all like football. If you're silly enough to admit you liked *When Harry Met Sally...*, you're going to be called a wimp, wuss, or

worse. But, in moments alone, you may actually discover that romance feels good, saying you care is great, and you don't have to be a macho idiot every moment of the day. If fact, being a true romantic is pretty manly.

6. Surprising a woman with a love letter disarms her. She's learned a series of defenses, both from her friends and from personal experiences with jerky guys. When you let her know you really care with a letter, she may respond in some very positive ways. (My wife sure did.)

The Medium and the Message

Understandably, the Internet offers us an easy way out. Entire courtships now take place on the Internet. While the jury may still be out when it comes to meeting someone special sight unseen, you can certainly use E-mail to correspond with someone you've just met to get to know him or her better. Humor and flirtation are easy ways to break the ice. You'll learn how to improve your E-mail writing skills just by reading this book.

You can create allure with a simple turn of phrase; be simultaneously mysterious and humorous; or come clean with your true feelings without stammering, stuttering, or "Um-ming." Communication can be fast and furious, or delayed and tantalizing, whether you use E-mail or snail-mail. Waiting for replies and conjuring your own letters is a passion sport.

There is, however, a case for sticking to the old-fashioned letter written on paper with a pen, and with a lot of thought put into it. A handwritten letter packs a bigger punch. You think through the sentiments you're committing to paper, and you neaten your penmanship. You're careful about mistakes. Even if you use block-letter print, your own handwriting is more personal than any typeface you could choose. Handwriting is intimate.

Even the process of writing out a love letter is romantic. I've known people who set their letter-writing scene with candles and music just as they would set the scene for an intimate evening with a lover. After all, your mood affects your inspiration and your words. Even the tools you use make a difference. Handmade paper can be more evocative than personal stationery and certainly beats out any old piece of paper. Your writing tool—ballpoint pen, roller-ball pen, or a special pen and ink—can make a real impact on your message.

Here's an example.

> *Dear Mary,*
> *I've been thinking about the last time we were together. I'd sure like to see you again. Soon.*
> *Yours,*
> *Rob*

Picture this message in three forms: E-mail, typed on paper, and handwritten.

E-mail is cool, a nice, safe message that could be about a business deal or a romantic evening. Typed on paper is also safe but is slightly more likely to be romantic—maybe urgent, maybe mysterious. Handwritten, though, this message is clearly mysterious, is compelling, and is likely to be passionate.

Understanding the medium and the message as separate ingredients can increase your letter-writing prowess. Consider a carefully handwritten note on special paper that poses the simple question, "What would you like to do tonight?" There's something touching and absolutely romantic in that gesture.

This works both ways, too. An E-mailed proposal of marriage is sadly diminished in its romance factor. Writing it down with a pen is practically like holding your loved one's hand. Your hand creates what his or her hand will hold. It's romantic.

What? Not the Romantic Type?

It's not all about flowery language or deeply felt intentions of commitment. There are countless methods of enticement and allure with words that seem completely harmless. Writing down what you want to say gives you more control to find your romance comfort level (but be sure to read this book so you write something worth reading!).

"Your eyes calm me."

Who could ignore this intriguing notion, borrowed from a Spanish phrase? Your love letters don't have to employ any hearts, flowers, or cupids to work.

"The only downside of kissing you is not being able to talk to you at the same time."

A few words can be a potent message. And light, flirty, romantic messages create intrigue and beg for answers.

"I don't need my 4 P.M. espresso when I hang out with you."

Try saying that out loud and you sound phony. Write it down and it's cool, intriguing, and more sincere.

Read on and you'll learn how to find your own romantic voice. Just as you have your own personality, you have your own way of writing down your thoughts, emotions, and wishes. You can try out different "voices" for your intentions, from classic to cool, abstract to hip-hop. You might not have considered the many options you have for "talking" in a love letter. You'll even have a chance to write some samples — for your eyes only — to get used to the whole process.

Once you feel more at ease with the whole idea of your own love letters and more experienced with your voice, you will learn to flirt on paper. Don't worry, you don't have to come up with all of your material. We'll help you with vocabulary, provide some tips on male-female communication, and give examples of how to reveal yourself in a letter. You'll be able to play with different levels of strength, enticement, and allure.

Seven Steps to Heaven. That's you.
If you don't get it, listen to it.

If you're into jazz you know that "Seven Steps to Heaven" is a famous Miles Davis piece. It's a complex, long, and involved musical selection that begs to be listened to many times, in many moods. This little love letter is a big compliment and says a great deal more than trying to describe the music — or the feeling you get from it — ever could.

For the first time in my life, my alarm clock is
my friend.
It reminds me of another day with you.

In a greeting card, this is a nice idea. On a piece of notepaper pressed into someone's hand, it's even more powerful.

Recently, my friend Jen went on a date with Bob, whom she'd met through a friend. They had a "nice enough" time but Jen didn't hear any bells or whistles. Bob, too, seemed pretty low-key and told her that he was leaving town on business for two weeks and that he'd call her when he returned. Jen figured that was a nice way of saying "don't hold your breath" and didn't expect to hear from him.

A few days later, in the mail Jen received a postcard with a photo that caught her eye: Elvis performing his act in Las Vegas in the early seventies.

> *Hi Jen.*
>
> *I had a great time with you last week and—I don't want to scare you but I've thought about you a lot since I left town. I hope we can get together again. Really, I'm not some psycho-stalker-weirdo on medication. I just have this feeling we could have something very cool.*
>
> *Bob*

This postcard brought Jen's interest and curiosity right back to the surface and made it an easy "yes" to another date. Was Bob an Elvis fan? Did he have a sense of humor she hadn't figured on? His "love letter" was simply a well-chosen, light way to tickle her interest. Smart Bob. He turned up the heat from their lackluster first date.

1

How to Find Your Romantic Voice

*She'll wish there was more,
and that's the great art o' letter-writin'.*

—CHARLES DICKENS,
THE PICKWICK PAPERS

*b*efore you put your hand to a pen, you must consider what you want to say, how you want to be "heard," and your comfort level with displaying your heart on paper. What I call your romantic voice is really a combination of three elements: structure, medium, and message.

For some of you, the structure of your letter

will come naturally, especially if you use basic letter-writing in everyday life. However, for those of you who didn't listen in English class and don't have to correspond much with the outside world, it's worth reviewing how to write a basic letter before setting off on your written romance.

Medium, too, is very relevant to your romantic voice. The choice of paper and ink, typed paper, or E-mail will have an impact on the message you write. Quoting Shakespeare in E-mail is less potent than writing the quotations out on handmade paper. Your romantic voice will shift and the power of your message will be (in part) determined by your choices. This will be discussed more thoroughly later in the book, but bear in mind that all is not equal in the realm of computer, typewriter, pencil, and pen.

Last, your message is obviously one that has to do with love, but how you come across, what you say, and how you say it are open for discussion. This chapter connects you with several rich modes of inspiration for finding, defining, and adjusting your romantic voice for every situation you encounter.

Please realize that you don't have to formulate your love-letter writing like a template for a business letter. In fact, you're best off using many different sources and resources for inspiration, to keep you fresh, interesting, and provocative. Love letters are strongest when written with real focus and intention for each occasion. In one case your words might be funny and cute, and in another deeply moving and intimate—both addressing the same person, but adjusting to different situations.

Keep your writing current by glancing back to this chapter for reminders of where new material can help you find the right romantic voice.

Framework for First-Timers and Beyond

Here's where knowing how to write a basic letter comes in handy. (There's a reason you had to sit through all of those classes on penmanship, composition, and grammar, and this is it.) You need to know certain rules, and then how to break them.

The basic structure of a classic love letter is obvious.

1. Dear You, (the greeting or salutation)
2. This is what I want to say. (the body of the letter)
3. Love, Me (the closing and signature)

A classic letter will always use these three components. Use the basic structure for the first letter you write, and in subsequent letters you can embellish the greeting and closing with personal flourishes.

Here is an example of a first letter.

Dear Susan,   <GREETING

Was it just me, or did something terrific happen last night?   < BODY

If it's just me, you should know you're making me crazy. I couldn't sleep when I got home. A simple night out doesn't ordinarily keep me awake, so it must have been something very new and different. I keep thinking about your smile, and the wonderful way you laugh.

I don't want to go overboard, but it would be great if you understand why I would say last night had a little magic in it, because if you do, it means you felt it too.

Thanks for a great evening. I hope there are more to come!   < CLOSING

Ralf   < SIGNATURE

After spending more time with the object of your affection, you can embellish.

My Dearest Kara,   <GREETING

Your presence in my life has changed the world around me.   < BODY

I know it because the grass is now much greener. My dreams are much sweeter. Even the dark and dreary days of winter seem filled with light. Thank you for saying "yes" last night and making me

Your loving husband-to-be, < CLOSING

Gary ✍ < SIGNATURE

You can see how the classic letter-writing structure can blossom with personal style as the relationship progresses. Ralf used a light tone for his initial contact with Susan, and Gary, his proposal having been accepted, let his happiness build up to the crescendo of his heartfelt closing.

When you're indecisive about your love-letter writing style, go with the classic; its structure and elegance will strengthen your message and lend you some graceful composure if you're feeling a little unsure.

Once you've gained more confidence—usually when you find yourself in a "conversation" with the one you love (or like)—you can experiment with more flip or avant-garde versions. Check out the examples below. Here the authors have side-stepped formalities and have shown their individual style. Most women like this kind of inventiveness coming from a guy. And I'm assured that men, while missing certainly subtleties, are just as easily touched by a message created specially for them. In the first example, you'll see a spare style that exudes a powerful message of "less is more." The second example lets us in on an "inside joke." Obviously, the writer found epithets an amusing way to communicate his admiration. And in the third example, the writer used a graphic device to help her make herself understood. Each is charming in its own way, and in the voice that reflects the author's personality.

You?
Amazing.
Me?
Confounded.
Us?
Beyond my wildest hopes.
Yours?
That's me.

Bike-peddling, tech-vest wearing, hand-holding, swing-dancing, style-setting, tasteless-joke-lovin' guy.

Meets kick-boxing, soft-sweater-wearing, cuddle-mongering, ballet-dancing, designer-dressing, giggling-at-jokes girl.

No way to describe the rest.

Love you.

Love
Is something
I never thought
Would ever happen to me.
But now that I've met you, it seems
I've reached that sacred place and I won't leave.

The Elusive Muse of Inspiration

Finding the way to talk on paper is not as easy as it sounds. Sure, you have more control. Sure, you can erase it at the last minute (then you have to start over). Where do you begin? You have that proverbial blank canvas in front of you.

Start with inspiration. If you're motivated to say something to someone, get down to that basic message and figure out the way it best sounds like you.

Even if your message is "thanks for dinner," if your heart wants to say something a little more poignant or passionate, here's your opportunity. After all, you can say "thanks for dinner" to your grandmother but it doesn't inspire a love letter.

Dear Tom,

*Last night's dinner was superb. It's an old saying,
but apt here: The company makes the feast.*

Thanks for such a special evening.

Teri

Teri used some help to get to this letter: her
inspiration came from *The Oxford Dictionary of
Quotations,* where she looked up "feast" and found
this proverb. Since it was only her third date with
Tom she didn't want to get too mushy, nor did she
want to be too cool. Here she found her comfortable balance between "I really like you" and not
coming on too strong.

Sometimes inspiration just hits you, and at other
times, like Teri, you could use some help. Don't
expect to do it all on your own. You don't have to.

Even if you want to say "Hi, I miss you," or
"Hey, it was nice to meet you," these simple little
messages can put out more energy and sizzle than
cordial, bland statements. You need to invoke your
romantic voice, and first you need to find some
source of inspiration to get it going.

MUSIC, MOOD, AND LYRICS

If music be the food of love, play on.

—SHAKESPEARE, *TWELFTH NIGHT*

Any teenager can tell you a major source of inspiration: music and lyrics. Music alone can set the mood to help you with your letter writing; relaxing jazz, classical compositions, even ragtime or polka music will shift the mood of your room and your own emotional disposition. Experiment with music to find the right piece to get your inspiration flowing, then let it rip.

Music with lyrics opens up more opportunity to express yourself. More than setting the mood, lyrics can provide a jumping-off point for your voice. Lyrics might offer help in phrasing just what you want to say, and your musical taste will also convey something about your personality. Are you more likely to quote Rodgers and Hammerstein, Frank Sinatra, or Prince? Do you feel inspired by modern alternative music, rhythm and blues, classic rock, heavy metal, rap, or colorful country and western? You probably could find inspiration in every one of these styles. Love is certainly expressed across all music, but the lyrics and the method might be very different. Reveal a little about yourself by your choice. Maintain some mystery: find a little-known song and quote something that touches you.

If you like the way someone else has said it, you can help yourself to a few lines or phrases that you admire. Best to credit the original author, though, so you don't end up looking foolish.

I get all choked up (still) listening to Simon and Garfunkel's "Kathy's Song"—and it immediately evokes a mood of deep intimacy, undying love, and melancholy.

If you're shy about borrowing words, try leaning into the mood of the music that speaks to you. You'll find your own voice once you've struck the right emotional chord. You're not just looking for sentimentality—not just for crooning, smooth love songs—but also for energy—alive and vibrant, or haunting, whispering, and amorous. Music from the past is ideal.

A rich vein of creative inspiration exists in the lyrics of music from decades before you might remember. Listen to music of the rich jazz and blues cultures that grew from the 1920s and thirties into the wartime hits of the forties. Take some time to explore old hits you never heard before. For starters, just listen to a few of these old hits. You'll get the idea.

DECADES OF MUSICAL INSPIRATION

1930s
"All of Me"
"You Made Me Love You"

1940s
"I'll Be Seeing You"
"Bei Mir Bist Du Schön"

"Sentimental Journey"
"Is You or Is You Ain't My Baby"
"It Was a Lover and His Lass"
"Blue Moon"
"Oh You Beautiful Doll"
"Again"
"That's My Desire"
"It's Magic"

1950s
"When I Fall in Love"
"That's Amore"
"Love Letters"
"She's Funny That Way"
"Memories Are Made of This"
"Let's Fall in Love"
"True Love"
"Nevertheless I'm in Love with You"
"Imagine"
"You Are My Lucky Star"

1960s
"Ain't That a Kick in the Head"
"Embraceable You"
"Love Is All Around"
"Do You Want to Know a Secret?"
"Maybe I'm Amazed"
"I Can't Believe You're in Love with Me"

A Note to Enthusiastic Female
Love-Letter Writers

In my experience, women relish composing a love letter with all its moody accoutrements. I had a friend who essentially consumed an entire evening with her love-letter writing, starting with a bubble bath, slipping into something silky that made her feel sexy, lighting a candle, and putting on romantic music. She wrote the most magnificent prose — creative, loving, deeply felt. Then she threw it away.

My friend was no fool. You can't pour your romantic soul into a love letter unless you know for a fact that the guy you are dating is going to be able to handle it. My friend knew that the guy she was writing to didn't have a clue that she felt so strongly and she got it out of her system by writing this huge romantic missive. After she destroyed what she'd written, she sat down and wrote a little note that carried much less weight: something more like, "Hey you, what's up? I'm dying to see the new Chuck Norris flick. How about you?"

If you're writing to your husband, go ahead and blather on with your romantic notions. No harm in overdoing it a bit. He might even be touched. But if you're just dating someone, be careful that mood and inspiration don't get the better of your common sense.

Girls, when you write a love letter, consider applying the same rule that applies to accessories: Just before you go out the door, take one thing off. Just before you seal that envelope or smack that "send" button, take one thing out of your letter (not the love). Part of provocative letter-writing is mystery.

While this isn't a hard and fast rule, if you're one of those women who love romance or who like to blend fantasy love with the real thing, beware of your ability to blow the guy away. One too many goopy sentences and your boyfriend might get the wrong idea.

A Note to Cautious Guys

Men, it's time to talk turkey. Be courageous with your creativity and you will be rewarded. I know this is tough.

Try to imagine that you're writing a hit song. Music lyrics take a lot of chances with emotion, and no doubt some of your favorite songs are good examples of love expression.

It's really worth trying to write this letter, and you can't make a mistake in trying to tell someone you love how you feel. Don't overthink it. Don't edit yourself. Don't show it to another guy. If you must get some help, show it to a trusted girl. She'll probably wish she was dating you.

Art is certainly a personal preference. It speaks to each of us with its own meaningful whispers. Your relationship to art can be very inspiring when it comes to writing your love letter. Here are some ideas you might not have considered.

Peruse old postcards, which are sold in many bookstores and flea markets. Scenes from resort towns or images of landmarks can provide a unique setting and springboard for inspiration.

Walk through a museum (I prefer the real thing, but I hear good things about virtual tours on the Web). Paintings can be very poignant, specific, and poetic. You might feel connected to some Old Master and use it only to evoke the mood you want to feel. *A Dance to the Music of Time* is a seventeenth-century painting by Nicolas Poussin that inspired the twentieth-century author Anthony Powell to use it as a title for his four-volume, twelve-novel series. Just think about that title in a love letter.

Being with you is a dance to the music of time.

It's totally unoriginal, but isn't it great?

Or, read about an artist you admire and see if history provides some interesting leap into your life. Then incorporate the image into your letter.

They say that da Vinci painted the Mona Lisa *with a loving brush. If only I could paint, you would inspire me to do the same.*

Art is a seriously undervalued source of inspiration (unless you're an artist or an art historian) in our society. There's classical art, with its sumptuous sculptures, marbles, frescoes, reliefs, and decorative scenes. Painting, too, from the caves to the canvas, provides a glimpse into passion and inspiration. Your taste, what you are drawn to, is all you need.

Art is very romantic. The idea of a passionate embrace was captured in the modern painting *The Kiss* by Austrian artist Gustav Klimt as well as in a sculpture called *The Kiss* by French artist Auguste Rodin. Almost any art history book will provide you with a panorama of works for your romantic eye. You might even incorporate a copy of the work in your love letter. A museum postcard with a passionate image on it would certainly convey a message without words.

Here some periods in art history famous for their portrayals of intimacy, along with one or more representational artists.

   ❧ Renaissance art—Botticelli, Titian, Correggio, Velázquez.

- ❦ Eighteenth-century French art —
  François Boucher
- ❦ Nineteenth-century French school —
  Bouguereau
- ❦ Impressionism and Postimpressionism
  of the early twentieth century — Monet,
  Manet, and Renoir

Be sure to check out local galleries, too. There are many talented artists around who might represent love or passion in a way that inspires you. Make use of your local library's art books, keep an eye out for them at flea markets. So many treasures of inspiration can be revealed if you just open your eyes. And your love letters will shine with personality and originality.

POETRY

If you're already wincing at the idea of poetry, cut it out. You don't have to dip into oft-quoted "How do I love thee" Browning sonnets to find something romantic. There are plenty of poets throughout the ages — including today's — from whom you can borrow some expression. Find something that touches you without seeming pretentious and you've found something you can quote and perhaps read aloud during a cozy evening with your lover.

Some people like old poetry.

Drink to me only with thine eyes,
And I will pledge with mine;
Or leave a kiss but in the cup
And I'll not look for wine.

—BEN JONSON (1573–1673),
"SONG: TO CELIA"

Angela,
You have vintage eyes.
Christopher

Poetry also helps you increase your romance level—and perhaps the surprise factor—even if you don't write it yourself.

To my Nan.
Lord Byron was talking about you when he wrote this two hundred years ago.

She walks in beauty, like the night
Of cloudless climes and starry skies;
And all that's best of dark and bright
Meet in her aspect and her eyes.
Always, your Joey

Kahlil Gibran's *The Prophet* is always a safe place to turn. His words are apt for many different occasions and are truly romantic.

Beauty is eternity gazing at itself in a mirror.
But you are eternity and you are the mirror.

Poetry doesn't have to be old, either. You can use some of the latest, hip new poets (they're getting a lot of media attention these days as well as corporate money to keep them writing). You can even paraphrase someone's poem or write your own. Here are some examples of poems that are more like inside jokes. You can do this, too. I know you can.

Ode to Sheila
You're my peanut butter. I'm your jam.
You're my honey roast and I'm your ham.
You're my pink and I'm your blue.
All this means is that I love you.

— JEREMY

How I Met Shermaine
By Linus
Blue.
Haze.

Who are you?

?

!

Cool.

Please don't be fooled into thinking that poetry has to be heavy, rhyming, romantic, and old-fashioned. There are so many ways to use poetry for inspiration. Take some time to look for something that appeals to you. Think about the joy your beloved would have reading some words you've chosen, or that smile you'd get for writing a little of your own verse. It's worth the risk. You never know, there might be a poet living beneath that resistant exterior!

LITERATURE

I know you read. After all, you have this book. Get out a few of your favorite books and see if there's a passage that inspires you. Start with what you know or admire, and go from there. You might find something that speaks to you through Hemingway, in a descriptive, deliberate, and careful prose. Or you might enjoy using more wild, rambling passages like those found in Tom Robbins's books. It would be foolish to try to list the many authors and sources available to you. Instead, you are best advised to go back and revisit a book that you've loved; perhaps you've read it more than once. Examine it; search for your favorite parts. Think about just what it is that makes this so interesting or special to you. Then share it in a love letter.

Like music, a passage of a book or story will reveal some aspect of your character you might find hard to put into words. Quoting literature is alluring and interesting and entices a conversation to be continued. You just might get a passage back and begin romantic correspondence with other people's words.

NATURE

Sublime feelings can be inspired by simple things: your favorite flower, a place from your childhood, or a view you shared with the one you love. This letter was written by a young husband to his wife, just after she gave birth to their first child, a daughter.

   Dear Pam,

It was less than a year ago when we sat together in Scotland, looking across the hills from that cozy glen, wondering if we would have a daughter or son. We have so much love. We are truly blessed.

And now we have our beautiful girl.

I'm so glad you want to name her Glenn. We will always remember that time and our love and her first days in our family.

I love you,

Bryant

Look to the seasons for inspiration, too. Each shift in our calendar brings its own flavor and accent to your relationship and your feelings.

Spring is the season most often associated with love, thanks to the exuberance of the growing season, new flowers, new life after the sleepy gray winter. Spring incites "get-up-and-get-out" energy that might help you write your first love letter or move your current relationship into deeper waters.

Summer is playful, too, but slower, more sensual. If your climate is hot, summer might inspire you to cool off, move more carefully and more purposefully. Find shade or respite; be cozy and cool. You can bare it all at the beach, or jot down some thoughts and entice a romantic encounter without revealing any skin at all.

Autumn offers infinite inspiration for love letters. Falling leaves, the first crisp winds of frosty weather, those autumn gray skies or ground fogs that are so romantic—it's practically a movie set. Take some of this feeling into your heart and let it come out in your writing.

Dear Alan,

I've always liked the fall. Crunchy leaves underfoot and wearing warm sweaters . . . the best part of all, though, is the great bonfire my folks have behind their barn on Halloween. This year I hope you'll be there, holding my hand.

Yours,

Becca

Your favorite season is the choice place to start. If it's winter, you can snuggle up with a quilt, some tea, and a pen to try your hand at intimate writing. When the weather keeps you inside, you might have time to write a love letter just for the heck of it.

Dear Gero,

I walked through the park today. The wind was so cold and the sun hid in the heavy clouds. But I thought of you and our early courtship — when we walked this same walk so many times holding hands. That kept me warm.

You're reading this while I make dinner. When I said "I love you" this morning, I really meant it.

Barrie

Summer's clouds, winter's frosts . . . nature's endless beauty supplies different ways to connect back to love. There are so many ways to express your love, your like, your intention. You need to find the best way for you. Practice as much as you like, try out different styles and see what inspires you. You don't have to account to anyone; this is purely your creative vein. I doubt any risk you take will be laughed at—quite the opposite, in fact.

      My Diane,

*   The mountains are white against this steel-gray sky. So cold, so unforgiving, but so alive, here—because I'm with you.*

*   Happy anniversary, ski bunny,*

*   Derek*

EXERCISE

To get you started with your writing, here are some sentences you can complete to remind you of what you want to say and how you want to say it. Do this exercise before you proceed with your letter:

1. I'm writing this letter because I _____

_____.

    (examples)

    A. had a great date

    B. want to see the person again

    C. want to apologize

    D. want to take the next step

E. want to say "I love you" in no uncertain terms

F. want to mark an occasion

2. The thing I admire most about the person receiving this letter is _____.
(examples)

A. his or her wit

B. his or her smile

C. the way he or she makes me feel

D. that I can trust him or her

E. his or her intellect

F. his or her lovemaking skills

G. that certain thing he or she does

3. The thing I want this person to know about me is that _____.
(examples)

A. he or she hurt my feelings

B. he or she made my day better

C. I really like him or her

D. I'm falling in love with him or her

E. I'm uncomfortable and want to slow things down, but not stop them

F. I can write a great letter

4. In this letter, the main thing I want to say is

_____.

(examples)

A. thank you

B. I'm sorry

C. I learned something new about you that I really like

D. I want to spend more time with you

E. I'm going to be really busy for a while; don't mistake this for a lack of interest in you

F. last night was special

G. I love you

5. I tend to be most inspired or moved by _____

_____,

so I should use that as my inspiration for my letter.

(examples)

A. music

B. movies

C. books

D. poetry

E. nature

F. art

G. conversation

H. prayer

6. My partner seemed to be most moved by _____

_____,

so I should try to incorporate that into my next
letter.

(examples)

A. music

B. movies

C. books

D. poetry

E. nature

F. art

G. conversation

H. prayer

2

The Art of Written Flirtation

*In the spring a young man's fancy
lightly turns to thought of love.*

—ALFRED, LORD TENNYSON,
"LOCKSLEY HALL"

*L*ove letters are not just for declarations of love, marriage proposals, or heavy-duty feelings of courtship. Love letters can also take on a lighter form—call them letters of like.

In our new world of electronic communication, written flirtation has become widespread, acceptable, and necessary to the beginning of most modern romance. We don't just flirt with our eyes, our hands, or our posture. We flirt through words.

Here is a glimpse of an E-mail flirtation conducted via Instant Messaging by a guy named BradNew5 and the recipient of his note, a girl named GlorGeous, whom BradNew5 had noticed in a chat room several times before.

> BradNew5: Hi GlorGeous. Do you live up to that name?
>
> GlorGeous: What do you mean by that, BradNew5? Do you live up to yours?
>
> BradNew5: GlorGeous—would be pretty, nice, and hot.
>
> GlorGeous: Okay, I'll buy that. But what's up with you?
>
> BradNew5: <<< not working at work. Just want to pass the time with some nice people. Everyone here is so boring.
>
> GlorGeous: Where is here? I'm goofing off, too.
>
> BradNew5: Newport Beach.
>
> GlorGeous: That's not far from here. Oops. Gotta go. Talk to you later.

You might think BradNew5 did some good flirting here, but he could have done a lot better. Here's an example of an improved flirtation with words. Again in Instant Message format, this conversation suggests improvements. Can you find them?

BradNew5: Hi GlorGeous. There's something about you that has me puzzled.

GlorGeous: What? Who are you?

BradNew5: I'm an admirer, I guess. We're in the same chat room.

GlorGeous: What puzzles you?

BradNew5: You seem nice. Mysterious. Different. Not like the typical dopes online.

GlorGeous: What makes you say that?

BradNew5: The way you take your time to answer, the way you write. You seem to think first. I admire that. I wish everyone in chat rooms were more thoughtful.

GlorGeous: That's nice of you to say. I have to run. I'll be here tomorrow.

BradNew5: Great. Speak to you then.

Are you wondering what was different here? It's simple. In the first exchange, BradNew5 performed an adequate conversation that went straight to his point, yet he was left wondering if and when GlorGeous would speak with him again. In the second conversation, BradNew5 was able to be more indirect, an effective flirtation device to promote interest, and the response he received proved successful: GlorGeous offered to talk to him again.

Flirtation Lesson #1

Write with indirect suggestion. Recall any situation in which you successfully flirted (and were flirted with), and you'll understand this notion. You don't walk up to someone in person and say "Hi. Where are you from? You're cute," unless you want to risk a huge brush-off. More often, successful flirtation involves baby steps to show your interest: meeting someone's eyes too long, brushing your hand across his or hers. These are indirect methods of establishing interest without hitting someone over the head with it.

The same goes for your writing. When you flirt with words, you don't want to be so blunt, but you don't have the subtlety afforded by standing physical proximity. You have to find a way to be subtle with your words. Flirtation is most interesting and compelling when it's not clear where it's going.

Flirtation Lesson #2

Establish your attractiveness with what you say.

BradNew5 would accomplish more if he became curious about GlorGeous. A statement like "You puzzle me" leads to curiosity. To ask a question compels an answer and begins the conversation. Compliments (but not too many) are pleasing.

There is no greater conversational bait than a question from someone who has both noticed and appreciated something about you. If you're standing there in person, you have more opportunity to establish conversation, but you need to choke up the courage to start. If you're online or you've met someone in person and want to follow up with a note, you can create magic with a mixture of curiosity and compliments. It's a delicate blend, though, so give yourself time to compose your words. Written flirtation is a skill that improves with practice but needs to be refreshed so you don't start sounding smarmy. Flirtation needs a two-party exchange; bait your conversational hook with something interesting.

Flirtation Lesson #3

Play with vocabulary.

Be provocative. Mysterious. Humorous. Tantalizing. Just don't be boring, mediocre, or flatfooted.

You can read, so you know what it's like to read something really dull. You certainly don't want to author anything boring if you want to be perceived as an attractive person. You don't have to be trapped into using large, long, intimidating words; just use words that aren't obvious.

Pepper your flirtations with unexpected or humorous or dramatic attempts to interest the object of your flirtation. Use words you hear, read, see, or imagine to get your written flirtations off the ground and out in the world. To help you out, we've compiled a starter list of questions and words for your reference. This is only a beginning, though, so don't lean on it forever.

Questions/Provocations for
E-mail Flirtation

What are you thinking about right now?

What is your greatest worry, and can I help you with it?

What are you reading these days?

I have an ethical dilemma; would you care to comment?

You seem to have a secret.

Are you always so sure of yourself?

There are an infinite number of ways to express yourself and your "like" without sounding obvious, mundane, or boring. It does get tiring, however, to constantly be trying to imagine more words, more descriptions, and more spice to add to your messages, particularly when you're in a hurry. To help you out, here are some vocabulary boosters for common expressions or feelings.

Words to Denote Your Interest or Like

take pleasure from	delight in	enjoy
have a weakness for	be fond of	desire
dote on	treasure	prize
think the world of	hold affection for	hold dear
enraptured	captivated	wrapped up in
enchanted by	mesmerized	hanging on words
pay mind to	fascinated by	spellbound
inspired by	rapt	drawn to
prefer	fancy	appreciate
choose		

Openers

Hi

Hey there.

Howdy.

May I introduce myself?

Pardon me, but I'd like a word with you.

Hello.

Please excuse the interruption but I'd like to talk to you.

I hate doing this but you seem so interesting . . .

I'm not good at getting things started, so please excuse me . . .

Words of Exclamation

Ooops!	Wow!
Zoiks!	Boy o boy
Awesome	Neat
Shucks	Swell
Gee whiz	!?!?!?
Boink!	Kerflooey

Tom met Karen at a friend's barbecue. He talked with her for a while but didn't have the courage to ask her out or to flirt very much. He kept that first conversation to the safe subjects of movies and music. Tom knew Karen's name and that she worked with a friend of his at an accounting firm. It didn't take a lot of effort to figure out her E-mail address at work, so he sent her a quick message to keep things moving. Knowing that personal E-mails might be against company rules, he wrote a careful, neutral message.

Hi Karen. It was nice to meet you at Ed's barbecue. Please could you E-mail me your home E-mail address? Thanks, Tom

Tom heard from her right away.

> *Hi Tom.*
> *I answer to KareBerrie@555.com.*

Armed with her home E-mail address, Tom composed this, his first official flirtation E-mail.

> *Karen,*
> *I have a weakness for girls who like Jackie Chan movies. Any chance you'll humor me and meet me for dinner this weekend? Maybe you could tell me the story of how a refined girl like you took the name KareBerrie online.*
> *Hope to hear from you.*
> *Tom*

I heard from a reliable source that Karen was tickled by Tom's interest and his funny E-mail. She liked the effort even though she thought he was a little corny. Here's what she wrote back to him.

> *Hi Tom.*
> *Glad you E-mailed me at home. My firm takes a dim view of employees admitting they have a personal life. Sure, I'll be happy to humor you over dinner. Could we do it on Thursday? I'm going away for the weekend. And, I have to know you a lot better before you find out the real story of KareBerrie.*
> *Karen.*

As you see by the harmless, low-risk exchange between Tom and Karen, they are interested in each other and have a flirtation already established. It didn't take a huge effort or put either of them in an awkward position.

If Karen had not wanted to see Tom, she could have easily slid out of it like this:

> *Hi Tom.*
>
> *Gads! You are a stitch. It was great talking with you at the barbecue. If it weren't for my pesky boyfriend I'd enjoy having dinner with you.*
>
> *See you at the next smokin' shindig at Ed's.*
>
> *Karen*

Since Karen and Tom have an established E-mail exchange, they will most likely "speak" to each other via E-mail to make their plans. Logistical conversations are often fertile ground for flirtation, but you can also go too far. By the time you meet in person, you might feel you know each other better. This is not always the best idea. E-mail exchanges will give you a false sense of intimacy if you carry on too much.

For flirtation and letters of like, less is more. Keep your E-mails light and airy, not dense and packed with details of your life. In example A,

Karen hits just the right note for a reply to Tom's next E-mail. In example B, she's overwritten.

✎ *Hi Karen.*
Thursday is great. Why don't I pick you up at your place at 7:30? I know a great little Cuban restaurant not too far away.
Tom ✎

Example A

✎ *Tom: 7:30 is a little early for me — can we make it 8:00? I love Cuban food and haven't had any in a while so that sounds perfect. Adios. K.* ✎

Example B

✎ *Tom: I won't get home until 7:15 because we have a conference call that usually goes late. Since I want to freshen up before dinner after my 12-hour workday, I'll need a little time to repair the mess. You could always come over early, though, and have beer. I don't mind if you can stand the mess. What do you think?*
K. ✎

Yikes. In example B, Karen did a good job of dismantling any abstract romantic illusions Tom might have harbored. Don't be lulled into E-mail slack. You want to be perceived as attractive, not wordy, neurotic, and tired.

1. **SHY GUYS:** There's a whole bundle of men who are absolutely crushed by rejection. It takes them forever to build up the nerve to approach a woman, and they turn away at the slightest sign of disinterest. To let this kind of guy know that you're truly interested involves using a very direct approach. This kind of fellow doesn't even take good hints.

For example, in high school, I had an unbelievable crush on a young woman whom I finally built up the resolve to talk to, in my own sweet, teasing kind of way. I often told her that her eyes always looked so sad.

In my high-school yearbook, she wrote, "Maybe someday you can show me how to make my sad eyes happy!" And I still never even asked her out. Years later, a teacher friend of mine confided in me that the girl had told him she couldn't believe I never called. Lots of you women call guys like me "losers," and maybe you're not too far from wrong. On the other hand, if you wanna see grateful . . .

Ladies, guys like me require a fairly direct letter, along the lines of, "I'd really like to go out with you. No, really. No kidding."

2. THE LADIES' MAN: This fellow is destined to sell life insurance, because rejection flows off of his back like water off a duck. He will, without a conscience, ask out anyone. His approach to dating is the old "throw it up against the wall and see what sticks" method. I used to really admire these guys. They wound up dating beautiful women, especially the ones shy guys (and even regular guys) couldn't bring themselves to ask out.

Most of you women, I suspect, are pretty wise to the Ladies' Man, so, if you see something in this person you like, or are intrigued by, a vague hint is all that's required. Letters to a Ladies' Man should be filled with intrigue and mystery.

3. CULT FIGURES: Sometimes a man can make great inroads with women simply by developing a "persona." Back in my day,

that meant being a long-haired "wow, far out" hippie type who was moody and troubled by the events of the day. Women swarmed to these guys like ants to honey. I hated cult figures, because they were the ultimate "gamers," who were willing to play roles that were so deceptive and insincere.

Flirting with cult figures is easy. Just play their game. This guy will use the persona act as long as it keeps working. Letters to him have to build him up, so you might not have the stomach to carry on a long correspondence!

4. REGULAR GUYS: Regular guys are those fellows who sometimes have nerve, and sometimes don't. They can be shy around startlingly beautiful women, but fairly comfortable around others. The "boy next door" type of guy is another category I wished I could have been when I was younger, but I just couldn't pull it off.

Handle regular guys with care. They hate being taken for granted, they hurt when they're rejected, and sometimes they miss out because you're so busy looking for someone a little more glamorous (see cult figure, above). Regular guys are probably a lot like you, a bit afraid and a bit bold, depending on the day.

Asking out a regular guy mostly means making it clear you're interested. You can't be too subtle or too pushy. Just write to him the way you'd like him to write to you.

Internet Language Shortcuts

I know that some of you are prone to using those adorable computer-chat-room shortcuts called Emoticons. Forget it. Even in a flirtation, you could look too lightweight, and besides, you might risk being misunderstood. Don't take chances with "E-mail art" when you're establishing your written interest. If you were using paper, I doubt you'd use little smiley-face stickers or other graphic nonsense. Unless you don't care or deliberately want to look a little cheesy (and this can be attractive to some people), don't do it. Leave it for the teenagers.

Avoid Emoticons

:) = Smiley Face	: D = Big Smile
: P = Sticking out Tongue	: o = Surprise
;) = A Wink	: (= A Frown
@-} — = A Rose	LOL = Laughing Out Loud
ROFL = Rolling on Floor Laughing	TIA = Thanks in Advance

This applies to those spelling shortcuts, too, like, 2hot2handle, or Bmine. Whenever you think about using something like that, think how you'd feel if someone sent it to you as a flirtation device. I'm not sure you'd think it sexy.

For colors and fonts, choose something that reflects your character and intention but be careful, again, of anything too strong. Heavy red gothic lettering is a bit much, but a typeface as pleasant as Palatino or as elegant as Caslon Open Face can say something about your style.

Taking big risks in shortcut language, color, and typeface is more of a teenage thing. If you are over twenty and you find yourself indulging in all of it, edit yourself now. There's a big difference between teen language (which is always changing and is an important code for them) and grown-up, sophisticated, real-world flirtation. Use whatever slang, colors, or fonts you want when you're talking to your friends or pretending to be young online, but do not toss your rich language and vocabulary skills overboard for it. It's just not sexy or appropriate.

Pen-and-Ink Flirtation

While the Internet may be the most-often-used medium for letters of like, there are still people who correspond with paper. Since, as previously determined, handwritten notes carry a lot of power and meaning, it takes a delicate hand to keep things light enough for playful courtship.

Dear Cyrus,

I liked what you did for the Boys' Wall of Fame at the Y. You brought a lot of people a lot of joy. Including me. How about sharing a cappuccino with me in appreciation of your heroic effort?

When would be good for you?

Betsy

Betsy used an opportunity to write a simple note of appreciation to Cyrus to begin a flirtation. Cyrus called her, as a result, and they continue to date.

Frank,

Basketball season is over. What are you going to do with all of that free time? Ever think of taking up hiking? It's a great feeling I'd be happy to share with you.

What do you think?

Talia

Talia's note is a little different. She had to use all of her courage to write to Frank. There was no way she could say anything in person, nor did she use the Internet. To keep things light, Talia chose an informal structure, and she used handwriting as casual as she could muster. True, Talia was heavily coached for this note and her friends had to work her over to get it written, but when Frank called and asked about a weekend hike, she knew the effort had been worthwhile.

Sometime pen-and-ink letters help the unsure hand feel more relaxed. Timid hearts can practice ways to approach someone they like and hone in on the way that works best.

Michael worked alongside Paloma every day in the same office. Although they didn't socialize, he knew that she was divorced and that she didn't have anyone special in her life. He always thought she was attractive, but he didn't want to risk getting turned down and still having to face her every day. Instead of a direct approach, Michael relied on an old grade-school standby: passing notes.

Note 1

Paloma,

Is it my imagination or is that new clock they installed a little slower than real life? I think it's really Friday, not Thursday.

Michael

When she received this note, Paloma smiled and looked up. Michael caught her eye and winked. A week later, he tried again.

Note 2

Paloma,

Any chance you want to do something different for lunch today? I'm going out for pizza (extra cheese and pepperoni). I'll get a large if you want some.

Michael

This time, Michael received his note back with this scribbled on it:

Yes yes yes! But no anchovies.

Two little light notes later, Michael had more confidence. He brought back a pizza and shared it first with Paloma before offering it others. His thoughtfulness was rewarded with a warm smile and, in his opinion, a quizzical look, as if Paloma were trying to figure out what he was up to. Michael took his time over his next move, but he decided to take another risk. The following week, he put note number three on Paloma's desk.

Note 3

Paloma,

There's a new restaurant at the mall that has a great happy hour. Some of us are going tomorrow after work. Would you like to join?

Michael

Michael had quietly organized a few friends to go out so he would feel more comfortable with this first pass. Paloma accepted readily, however, and Michael thought there might be some interest on her part, too. He knew for sure when he received a note on his desk.

Michael,

There's a great new action movie at the Strand. The six-o'clock show on Friday is half price. My treat if you're interested.

Paloma

Michael's heart melted with Paloma's offer, and he accepted the invitation. They continued their note exchanges as they began to date, and they are now in a committed relationship.

For timid hearts, it's best not to go too fast. Michael found the note-passing scheme easy because it was so casual. If you can't pass notes, there are other ways to keep things light:

- ✒ Send a greeting card with a funny image
- ✒ Pass along a magazine article or newspaper clipping that might be of interest
- ✒ Give a little present with a note
- ✒ Write a note of appreciation, thanks, or admiration for something the person did.

Your notes of flirtation can only improve with practice. You can also show your efforts to a friend for advice, which is not necessarily something you'd do with a deeply personal love letter. It's always useful to find someone of the opposite sex (if that's what you're after) or a friend of your intended recipient (if that friend can keep a secret) just so you can get some feedback.

Otherwise, the tried and true method for self-editing and getting it just right is this:

The Art of Written Flirtation

1. Think about what you want to say.
2. Say it (write it down).
3. Read what you wrote.
4. Make any changes.
5. Read it again.
6. Leave it for at least twenty-four hours (this is a "cooling-off period" that will allow you some perspective and adjust your comfort level).
7. Read it again.
8. If approved, send it.

Most likely, you'll want to agonize a little. This is absolutely normal; after all, we're talking about matters of the heart. If you really like someone and you want to extend yourself through a note, you're perfectly within your rights to be nervous and to take into consideration exactly what you want to say.

Review this chapter whenever you come across a new love opportunity and want to try your hand at written flirtation.

3

Courtship: Building Your Romance with Letters

Love bears all things, believes all things, hopes all things, endures all things.

Love never fails. Where there are prophecies, they will fail, where there are tongues, they shall cease, where there is knowledge, it shall vanish away.

For we know in part, and we prophesy in part, but when that which is perfect comes, the imperfect will go away.

*When I was a child, I spoke like a child,
I understood as a child, I thought as a
child, but when I became a man, I put
away childish things.*

*For now we see through a glass dimly,
but then face to face. Now I know in
part, but then I shall know even as
I am known.*

*And now these three things abide,
faith, hope, and love, but the greatest
of these is love.*

—I CORINTHIANS, CHAPTER 13, VERSES 4–13

*I*f you've mustered at least a little confidence at this point, you'll find this chapter will stretch you even further. Flirting is fine: it's playful, safe, and easygoing. When flirting shifts into a more substantial relationship, however, your words begin to count more heavily and the stakes will feel higher. Just when you feel you have a grip on writing letters of "like," the desire to go deeper can give you an abrupt case of the jotting jitters.

Going Deeper than Flirting

No one can put his or her finger on that exact moment when a recreational flirtation becomes more serious sport. For some people, a few dates in person establish a connection that immediately seeks deeper romance. For others, an entire year can pass before any substantial emotional revelation occurs. Most likely, you find yourself somewhere in the middle, needing a bit of personal time and distance to determine when flirtation shifts to romance, when like turns to love. It may even vary by relationship.

What matters most at this point is being able to say what you feel, feel what you say (two different things), and listen to the responses you receive.

Dear Chad,

You're a stitch. I'm still smiling about last night. I never knew someone so "banker" could be such a comedian. You surprise me in so many ways. I hope you find me surprising, too.

Yours,

Hannah

Dear Hannah,

I'm surprised that you laugh at my jokes.

See you soon,

Chad

Hannah was wondering if growing feelings for Chad were going to be reciprocated. In this note to him, she was clever about "testing the waters." First, she used E-mail to make her message less "heavy," and second, she implied a tiny bit of intimacy with her words. Chad could have responded with a cozier note complimenting her on something, but instead he chose to keep the distance with a joke and the more remote closing, "See you soon." Chad's response told Hannah to keep things light.

There are other ways of "fishing" to get to the next level. Metaphor works wonders.

Dear Talullah,

The amount of wine consumed last night was less than a bottle, but today I still feel intoxicated. Clearly this was a vintage evening. I'd like a case of them, please.

Robert

Dear Robert,

I happen to have a large inventory of that particular vintage and hope that it will accommodate your needs.

T.

Robert and Talullah converse in a metaphor about wine (this is not an original idea) and manage to convey, without any sloppy sentiment, that they like each other. Talullah also uses a subtle technique that invites intimacy: using only her initial to sign off. This is the beginning of a cozier, private exchange.

   Dear T.,

Glad you can accommodate the need. I was thinking of a weekend worth, for now. Would you care to be my escort to the Air Show this weekend and perhaps stay the night in a little B&B I know by the sea?

Separate rooms, of course.

R.

   Dear R.,

Regrettably, I have plans with my visiting family (my Midwestern roots have decided to pick up and come here for the weekend). We will have a very casual brunch on Sunday at the barbecue place on Main Street if you would care to join us. The folks are perfectly nice and respectable but sadly, not the same vintage. You will not be reprimanded if you decline.

T.

   Dear T.,

I feel up the challenge and will be most charming, if that's at all possible, on the condition that you give me your first night free after they depart.

R.

Dearest R.,

You are a champ. Details to come.

T.

P.S., Tuesday is yours.

As the above correspondence illustrates, flirting and suggestion can easily shift into a deeper emotional connection. There is so much gray area concerning the transition from flirtation to romance that the testing grounds will largely depend on your own comfort level. Taking a chance with a more intimate communication doesn't have to hit anyone over the head. You can be subtle, humorous, or ticklish:

- Use a nickname that may have cropped up in flirtatious conversation. *"Hey ChubLubber, How about an away game? My place, Saturday."*
- Ask lightly about getting together in a romantic situation. *"Have picnic basket, prize-winning chicken-wing recipe, and best lemonade this side of paradise. Are you up for a picnic?"*
- Give corny compliments. *"You are crack-the-whip smart and golly-gosh-darn if you aren't a looker, too."*
- Confide something important but not too personal. *"I think you're the only person who has ever*

really understood both my sense of humor and my fears. Are you sure you're human?"

Another reason to keep things on the light-and-fishing level is to ascertain how you really feel. You might have waves of like-love-fear and want to back off at first, and moving slowly with your correspondence is one way to prevent feeling as if you're in over your head. The trick to finding the right depth in romantic waters is to fish. Use bait that isn't embarrassing or too revealing, then carefully read the response you receive.

Understanding Responses

It bears mentioning that conversations are two-sided and that, while you hope to communicate something on your end, your message may be received in an entirely different way. The rule of communication is as follows: *It's not what you say but how it is heard.*

Written communication has its drawbacks when it comes to the tricky area of being emotionally understood. Words you write may seem more harsh, more intimate, more tender than you intend them to sound, simply because you don't have the opportunity to give them your voice's inflection. Your reader might think you're very bold if he or she doesn't read the humor in your words. (Emoticons can be used to inject the humor button here :), but only as a last resort.)

The only way you'll know how well you're communicating your intention is to read the response. If you surmise that there's some confusion, there probably is. If you think you've scared him off, counter it with a light tone. If she sounds angry, ask if there's something bothering her. Fish until you find the right depth.

Ultimately, though, you may receive a response that essentially communicates "not interested." In this case, bow out gracefully, take some time to recoup, and get back out there to your next flirtation. Whatever you do, don't fall into a trap of reading between the lines or trying to find meaning in being brushed off. Your love letters and flirtations may be fabulous but the person you wrote them for may not be.

1. Yourself

   As much as you might think you need to reflect some kind of image—whether it's surfer dude or super-intellectual—you will be most successful by being who you are. If that means short, terse sentences and little description, that's fine. Who you are should come out in your letters, not someone you can't live up to.

2. Fun

   Sure, women like a good joke, play on words, and teasing as much as you do. Just don't go too far, get gross, or push into areas in which you haven't yet established where the line is drawn. Your idea of fun might be her idea of bad taste.

3. Innuendo/Hints

   Mystery and hints work well for provoking curiosity and building up your next date. Be sure to have something to reveal or give, though, because she'll take you at your word when you say you have a surprise, and if there is no surprise, don't be surprised if she splits.

Don't Go Here

1. Lying
   Better not to say anything at all than
   something you don't mean.
2. Whining or Manipulation
   No one likes a love letter that's really
   complaining about how you're not perfect or manipulating you to go somewhere you don't want to go. (No: "I
   would just love to see your golden hair
   flying behind you as we cliff dive into the
   blue Caribbean sea—you'd look so beautiful in the air."
3. Other Women
   It's NOT a compliment to say, "Of all the
   women I've known, you're the best in
   bed." Ugh.

What a Guy Likes in Writing

1. Fun

   Good times shared are great for romance, and thanking him for showing you a good time is a great way to fuel your connection. Tell him you're open to more adventures.

2. Common Interests

   Your letters can probe for those shared passions, or remind him that you like doing lots of the same things he does. Feeling as if you're on the same team builds a sense of partnership.

3. Sexual Intimacy

   Taking the next step sexually is one of the more obvious signals things are getting serious, unless, of course, you've been on the fast track already.

   Conveying the importance of this area is tricky. You don't want to come on too strong, but, if becoming more intimate is meaningful and important to you, it's only fair to let him know. He shouldn't toy with your feelings any more that you should hide yours from him.

   Be gentle; say something that makes him know that you're into him.

Don't Go Here

1. Nagging
   Never nag in a love letter. Enough said.
2. Jealousy/Possessiveness
   It's unattractive in person. In writing, it makes you seem insecure. No "I was so disappointed that I couldn't find you for that last dance," either—that's manipulative and we see through it.
3. Commitment Pressure
   If it doesn't work in person, why would it work in writing? Ultimatums, too, can be dangerous if you're not willing to go through with the "or else" bit.

Getting Deeper

Once you do have a sense that your flirtation is finding new connection and depth, becoming intimate and broaching the like/love threshold, your writing will change it's direction. Passion and eroticism may permeate your written relationship. Sure, it's not mandatory, but when you fall in love, all

sorts of nonsense likes to make its way onto paper.
And you should enjoy every morsel.

   Dear Roseanne,
I think I just learned what "intimate" means.
Love, Tom

   Dear Lisa,
   When a sailor is out to sea a little too long, he
begins to think about finding a safe harbor. In the shelter
of a cove, the battering storm subsides and all peril goes
away, at least for a time.
   I am not a sailor. But you have become my safe
harbor. Holding you shields me from the worst storm
life can dish out. I hope you know how much that means
to me.
   Love,
   Art

   Dear Sophie,
   There are so many writers who describe making love
as a form of "surrender." They are so wrong. You have
taught me that sharing yourself is not a surrender: it is
a gift. This gift is one I accept with wonder, and awe.
Your passion and compassion are gifts I will always
treasure, whether we are together forever or only this one
time. What we shared last night is now a part of me.

It may not be wise to tell you I have been moved so much by our time together. Still, I must, to be honest with you, and with myself.

I will be thinking of you, until we are together again.

Bill ✍

Writing these first letters beyond the like/love border is important. They just might be an archive of the romance that brings you a long-lasting, permanent relationship. These letters are revealing, exciting, and often titillating communications that mean something only to the two of you, a budding new couple.

You still don't have to use the big "L" word, either. In fact, it may be best to keep the desire to say "I love you" under wraps, for now. It's simply too easy to explore and write about your feelings in other ways. When you fall in love, every single mundane thing in life can look new, more vibrant, more beautiful. Reveling in the details of everyday life can build a connection between you in unusual and highly personal ways.

✍ *Meine Liebe,*

You obviously have time for no one but me since you left your watch here. A hostage now, until Saturday.

XXOO Barrie ✍

I have a volume of E-mail conversations that evolved over the first three months of my relationship with my husband. Above is one of the shortest and least descriptive, but they range from our mutual taste for peas and carrots to daily installments about our personal trials and tribulations. In a totally romantic gesture, he had the E-mails printed out and bound by a professional bookbinder and presented them to me at our three-month anniversary.

Not only did my then-boyfriend, now-husband, sweep me off my feet, but we read bits of this early exchange every year on our anniversary. It's wonderful just to giggle and be reminded of that scary, passionate beginning. I can't believe how every tiny thing we did seemed so funny and interesting—and how much fun we had bantering. This written deepening of feelings and flirtation led to slowly revealing ourselves and gradually led to quite serious love letters—the kind I'm entitled not to share.

Once you have established banter with someone you care for and who is also fond of you, enjoy yourself. Take risks when you want to, be more measured when you don't. These beginning love letters are pivotal exchanges, in which you have nothing to lose by revealing exactly who you are. You stand to be loved and appreciated and your letters can help you get there.

    Dear Otto,

    *It seems as if every week only has three days in it —
the days I see you. All the other silly days are
unnecessary, badly distributed wastes of time.*

    Don't you agree?

    *I have a yen for sushi tonight. Love it if you'd saki-
it-to-me. (Couldn't help myself.)*

    Adele

    Yenful Adele:

    *Had sushi for lunch. Would you care to take a rain
check and head farther east for Chinese? I have a calling
for Buddha's Delight. Of course, his delight is nothing
compared to yours.*

    O.

It's up to you to decide how much of your personality to evoke with tone and humor. Some written conversations include private language, baby talk, foreign language, or shortcuts that mean something only to you. The process of your letter writing has its own energy and timing. Everything means something, especially silences.

Steamy Missives

Romance takes its own time and has its own style with every couple. If you're writing part of your romance into love letters, you're bound to wander into descriptive, sensual, or passionate occasions. Some of you will excel at this, musing over a caress, a kiss, an embrace. Perhaps you'll find there's a bodice-ripping rogue in your writing, suggesting far more on paper than you would be able to suggest in person. There is no right or wrong way to go about this. It's more important to be yourself and let your words and sentiments evolve naturally. Yet, if you're timid or unsure of how appropriate it is or how far to go, take it easy and start slowly.

A simple kiss has been the inspiration for end-less poetry, songs, paintings, plays, and operas. Kisses can be scandalous and stolen, chaste and dainty, as well as deeply passionate. Kissing is an ideal subject for your first letters of passion.

Ernest, a self-described shy bookworm, was particularly proud of the way he handled the courtship of his wife, Jennifer. When they met, Ernest lived two hundred miles away from her; he knew he liked her right away and began a corre-spondence with typed, mailed letters. They saw each other once a month, and after the first two months, Ernest sent Jennifer this poem.

> *Jenny kiss'd me when we met,*
> *Jumping from the chair she sat in;*
> *Time, you thief, who love to get*
> *Sweets into your list, put that in!*
> *Say I'm weary, say I'm sad,*
> *Say that health and wealth have miss'd me,*
> *Say I'm growing old, but add,*
> *Jenny kiss'd me.*

—LEIGH HUNT, NINETEENTH-CENTURY GUY
  WHO KNEW HOW I FEEL

When Jennifer received this poem in the mail, she knew that Ernest was someone she wanted to spend a lot more time with. She responded with this, the first handwritten note she would write to him.

> *Ernest,*
> *My lips are waiting for their next encounter with yours. Until then,*
> *Jen*

Jennifer gave a green light for intimate communications but didn't take it too far. Ernest felt emboldened by her response and carefully stepped up his writing. Since he's shy, Ernest shared only this passage:

> . . . *Holding you in my arms was like fitting that elusive, missing piece of me back in where it belonged. When I leave you, my arms feel lost. When I think if you, my heart is full and my body is alive with fire . . .*

Ernest treasures the passionate letters they exchanged in their courtship. He now considers himself highly passionate and romantic, characteristics he never knew he had.

There are ample opportunities for you to explore your budding passions in writing, too. Part of the fun is seeing who you are in your words, exploring your talent to describe passion and defining who you are as a couple.

Dear Delores,

When I woke this morning, I was almost angry, because I wasn't ready for last night to end. Being with you touches me in ways I cannot fully describe.

Your softness is like nothing I have ever known. The gentleness of your touch, the feel of your body, the sensation of being up against you arouses me even now, as I write these words.

When we are intimate, the rest of the world goes away. I feel only you. I breathe only you. I sense only you. Making love simplifies my purpose in life to its glorious best: trying to satisfy you and to make you feel the ecstasy that encompasses me. Making love with you reduces my needs to one: to savor what you give.

Before being with you, I had heard of passion and seen it in movies; I was a witness to something I thought was faked. Being with you means I now know how real passion can be. You have opened your heart, and opened the gate to a new world for me. Did you know you had such a power?

I will live with a hunger, and a thirst, from knowing you. I will hunger for your body, and thirst to drink from the fountain of desire that you inspire in me, for as long as I live. Only you can quench my thirst, and feed my hunger, even as the craving grows stronger with each passing day.

Please forgive my foolish words. Accept them as tokens of the emotions you inspire in me. I will wait anxiously to be with you again. Until then, you will live in my heart, and in my memories. I will ache with a yearning that can only be satisfied by kissing your glorious lips and touching your exquisite body.

Love you. Jim.

Julie,

My life is starting to become different, even if my days seem the same. And I must confess that it's you who has changed my outlook. You have opened my eyes to some amazing new possibilities. Your touch is so gentle, *your kisses are so delicious, and your body is soft when it presses against me. I will forever be filled with a new sense of wonder and joy, because you have shared these things with me.*

I must confess that in some ways I feel inadequate. Can I match your gentleness? Can I give any feeling as warm and secure as the one you have bestowed on me? You have chosen to show me such strong passion combined with such sweet affection, and I can only hope you feel a glimpse of the same from me.

Our time together is very special. There are very few moments that a man knows will linger with him for the rest of his life, and you have already given me many. Thank you for being such an extraordinary part of my life. I hope we will continue this journey together for a long time to come.

John

While erotic writing is not what this book is about, you might want to explore some authors who do it rather well. Books by famous romance writers are excellent in describing passion; and there are even books on the vocabulary romance writers use to define various embraces, body parts, and activities. You might find sources like *The Literary Companion to Sex*, by Fiona Pitt-Kethley, helpful, if not downright inspiring. History provides us with ample citations and some ancient, graphically described sentiments; if you're reluctant to indulge in steamy, suggestive romantic writing, your ancestors were not!

Don't Do This

By example instead of by instruction, here are things to avoid. Clumsy writers who didn't mean to come off so badly wrote these letters. Their names are changed to protect them from obvious criticism.

Dear Ernestine,

I've been thinking about last night, and I've decided you're really hot. So, we'll do better next time, even though this one wasn't so great. I know you got it in you.

When I told my friends what a great kisser you were, they reassured me you could do everything else well, too. I really dig you, so I want to keep trying.

You know I'll always respect you. Let's just think of this as a little bump in the road, if you know what I mean.

Love,
Landis

Dear Jerry,

You're my dream come true. I love the way you look at me. I love sitting in your convertible, and holding your

hand under the table. I think we're perfect for each other.
Our kids will be so beautiful.

If you're wondering, I like emerald-cut diamonds and
my birthday is coming up!

Love, Krissy 🐝

Both of these letters come off badly because they're too obvious. Landis breaks every rule in the book. By saying something as arrogant and unromantic as "I've decided you're really hot," he almost begs Ernestine to reply, "Well, you're really NOT." And citing his discussion with friends about their shared physical activity is practically a romantic felony. Forget writing any letter at all if you like this style.

Krissy breaks a rule more commonly associated with women (but certainly not limited to them): getting too close too fast. You wouldn't know that this was written after their third date. She also speaks more about things (cars, diamonds) than about her feelings for Jerry. Even if this were written after a yearlong relationship, Krissy comes off shallow and vulgar.

Declaration of Love

If all goes well, at some moment in your life you will write a love letter as a prelude to a committed romantic relationship, or you will reach a moment in time that cements feelings for eternity. Whether or not your relationship lasts, the feelings you want to share are awesome and should be treated with eternal respect. A declaration of love, on paper, is a valuable document that may last forever.

How on earth can you live up to something so huge and meaningful? The very thought of writing a letter that someone might keep forever — or that generations to come will read and wonder about — is far too daunting. Maybe Shakespeare could do it, but you? Sure you can.

Don's Letter-Writing Campaign

When I started courting Pam, one of the first things I found out about her was that she loved deep bass voices. Unfortunately, I don't have one. Since I didn't want to lose out because of being vocally challenged (I

---

sound a lot like Ted Turner, which isn't exactly sexy), I needed some other outlet. I've always liked to write.

Pam is an easy subject to write about. For one thing, she's beautiful. I can start from the top and work down, or from the bottom and work up, and I'd have a rich variety of physical features to sing praises about. So, I never did. I figured she'd had enough guys telling her how gorgeous she was/is. Instead, I wrote to her about the other kinds of beauty she displayed.

First, she loves her family. I've always known I couldn't fall in love with a woman who ignored her family. Pam's warm affection for her parents, brothers, and sister was very attractive. A loving family often leads to another loving family.

Next, Pam has a passion for life. When we met, she had recently moved to the Midwest, with her own contagious joy in living. She could take a matter as simple as singing a song and make it into great fun. Every time I would spring a new event on her (how about taking her on a date to see a Kansas City Royals baseball game, three hours away?), she would respond with incredible enthusiasm. What made it even more special was that, at the time, I was a poor grad student living on very little money. Pam could take a night filled with a six-pack on her front porch and turn it into an evening to remember.

In other words, the inspiration part was easy.

The first time I wrote Pam a love letter was after I knew I was already hooked. Being a writer at heart, I finally decided to put a few things down.

My letters were passionate, mushy, and dripping with the angst of a guy who knew he was in love but wasn't sure how it was all going to turn out. Pam wasn't looking to get involved with any one person, and she had made that very clear. I can't say my letters won her over, but each time I sent her one (I'd leave them on her porch, or give them to her in person just before I'd head off to class), she responded with great affection. That just made me want to do it again.

I probably wrote Pam a dozen letters or so, over the next few months before we were married. She keeps them in a safe place, and I haven't asked to see them.

What is fascinating to me is how things evolve over time. Pam and I have been married for over twenty years. We have three children and two grandchildren. Even now, we exchange little notes. E-mails and letters are part of our continuing courtship. Pam signs her notes, Meee . . . , as a small gesture of affection.

The trick to writing a really good declaration of love is not to think about it at all. Just write with your heart. Write what you feel, how you love. There's no match for talent when your heart is doing the talking.

My dearest Skip,

When I was thirteen, I saw you for the first time standing on the pier securing your dear old sailboat. I remember thinking you were the dreamiest dreamboat I had ever seen.

At the time you were with someone else, and I wasn't even on your sonar. But now, almost twenty years later, I still look at you and tingle from your handsome smile.

And best of all, you see me as someone to trust, to confide in, to play with, and to enjoy life with. You make me so happy. I can't begin to describe how I feel, so I'll just offer this: I love you.

Ever dreaming of you,
Karen

Dear Pickle,

Things are just not the same anymore. I don't sleep well; I don't really concentrate on life the way I used to. My bowling score is down; I never see my friends, and the last time I went to a movie I saw a chick flick. I blame you.

Sorry, but you've intruded long enough. I have to put an end to this. I think we should get married. I love you (as if it isn't obvious).

Fishman

More Good Examples

Try something like these. Here are several letters of romance and love declarations that can give you a feeling for different styles and levels of romance. They have been written by both men and women to give you a broader perspective. Don't be fooled into thinking men can't write good love letters.

Frankly, I've seen some pretty stunning examples from guys.

> Colleen,
> Where did you find that perfume? When I woke up this morning the scent was all around me, and I became intoxicated by it once again. How can one woman and one aroma bond together to drive me so wild?
>
> Or, maybe it wasn't fragrance. Maybe the scent only reminds me of how good things felt in our time together. Maybe I'm waking up to discover that you are becoming special to me. Maybe the chemistry is more than cologne.
>
> There is only one way to sort out this mystery. We need to be together again. Please help me understand what is happening. We need to figure out how it is that you are able to cast such a spell over me. If you're ready for the journey, send me the signal. Wear the same perfume, or just say the words. Either way, I'll be vexed and perplexed until we see each other once again.
> Michael

> My Dear One,
> I'm in a place. It's a place I've never been before. This place is calm and serene, but exciting and exhilarating, all at the same time. This place is neither a

state of mind nor just one of physical being. It is a place where my soul soars. It is the place I share with you.

I'm in a place where my mornings begin with you in my thoughts, and my days end with you on my mind.

I'm in a place where, when good things happen, my first reaction is that I'm thrilled, because I'll get to share them with you.

I'm in a place where, when bad things happen, I know you'll be there to provide comfort and make the world right again with a simple smile, or with a soft caress of my hand.

This place that you hold in my heart is precious beyond words. You are there, and I am a better man because of it.

When I hold you in my arms, I'm in a place that I never want to leave. It's a place that I pray you will wish to stay.

I love you,
Don

Marius,

The sea that parts us is my enemy, but I gaze at the moon and ask it to reflect my love back to you so far away.

You are the answer to my passion and my life dreams. I live for seeing you again, for being whole with you again. Now that you've given me the luscious gift of your love, my appetite is endless.

I miss you, my dear. I look to September as the only page of the calendar that is my friend.

Je t'embrasse avec tout mon coeur.

Adrienne

Judy,

It's confession time. I am struggling with something new, and so awesome. I struggle with this, because I know there is a risk involved when you tell someone how you truly feel, especially when those feelings run as deep and as wide as the ones I have for you.

What should I say? How should I say it? I don't know for certain how you will respond. I can only wonder if you share these same emotions.

I care so much about you. What we have is like holding a small, frail, newborn creature. It needs nurturing. It needs tenderness. It demands caution. It is so precious.

And so, I wonder, and I wait. I want you to know what is in my heart. Yet I remain frightened. Do these thoughts seem familiar to you? Perhaps when we are next together, we should talk about them, carefully.

Just know for now, that when I hold you in my arms, I am in the safest, most treasured place in the world. I dream the same is true for you.

With love,

Max

Courtship: Building Your Romance with Letters

Erin,

Here's how I know I love you:

1. Food tastes better.
2. Wine tastes sweeter.
3. I notice flowers.
4. I can't stop thinking about you.
5. Sex doesn't sound right. Lovemaking does. And, all those other adjectives I used before now just sound kind of gross.
6. When something good happens, you're the first person I want to tell.
7. I dream about you, and wake up very happy.
8. I drop your name to everybody I know. Maybe it's because I want to make sure they know we're together.
9. I'd rather be with you than with my buddies. How is that possible?
10. You can put me in a good mood in a flash.
11. I sit in my office and try to think up new ways to compliment you.
12. People tell me I look good, as if I've lost weight or something. I have. I've lost the weight of feeling lonely and alone.
13. I don't cringe at the idea of meeting parents.
14. I wonder what it would be like to have kids.
15. I can visualize you in a wedding gown.

How to Write a Love Letter

Will you marry me? (I'm going to know in a second, when you look up from this letter and see the ring I have in my hand.) Cool, huh?

Adam

At this point, your romantic voice and vision should take over. When you tell him or her that you're in love, do so with your heart and write with the confidence that only love can bring.

4

Occasional Letters

You say me-wards your affection's strong;
Pray love me little so you love me long.

—ROBERT HERRICK, "HESPERIDES"

*W*riting a love letter to declare your amorous intentions is only the beginning of your love-life archive. Life doesn't stop when you get married or enter into a long-term commitment, nor does letter writing. You can find so many occasions to write love letters that it could be a part-time job. Once in a while, a little note can pick up your intimacy level just as a big, juicy love letter can mark an occasion. You be the judge of what to write; just be sure to keep writing.

The Obvious Occasions

MARRIAGE PROPOSAL

Once you've made your commitment as a couple, you could each write a letter to make the occasion really memorable. Such letters may even become part of the archive you will someday share with your children. Peter and Barbara marked their official engagement with these letters.

> *Dear Peter,*
>
> *I can hardly catch my breath, I am so filled with surprise, excitement, and anticipation of our union! I am so happy, and I hope so much that you will always be happy to call me your wife.*
>
> *Reverend Willis says that marriage is a blessed state, and I believe so strongly that he is right.*
>
> *I know we are blessed in the life we can build together, and the children who I hope will call us Mom and Dad.*
>
> *I love you,*
> *Barbara*

> *Dear Barbara,*
>
> *I know it sounds corny to say that you've made me the happiest man in the world, but I guess you're marrying an old cornball.*

Every day from now on, I will think of the world in
terms of "us," our family, our lives together. Sometimes
it's a little scary, but mostly it's exciting. Let's always
remember this time.

   Love,
   Peter

WEDDING DAY

Just like the beginning of an engagement, your
wedding day is an opportunity to capture a very
special moment on paper. You'll feel extraordinary
on that day—alive, bright, sometimes even sur-
real—with your family and friends surrounding
you in support of your union. People weep at wed-
dings under the spell of that intense emotion, and
no photographer, video camera, or witness will be
able to preserve that feeling as well as your own
words will.

   The following notes, written by brides and
grooms, will give you an idea of what you can write
on your wedding day.

   Elfrieda found this note in the florist's box
when her bouquet was delivered.

   Darling E.,
   You know that I hate being in the spotlight and
would gladly bag the wedding in favor of a Las Vegas

chapel. But for you, I will be the proper groom today. And tomorrow, I will only be your husband, a role I will play without effort or sacrifice.

I love you, E.,

Happy Wedding Day,

F.

Fred was given this note by one of his grooms-men while they waited for the bride to arrive at the church.

Dear Almost Husband,

I asked Tad to give you this note just before I see you at the church, in your final moments of "single-ness." I just want you to know that I will do my best to make you happy, and that I love you with all my heart. Whatever life brings us, I will make the best of it, for better or worse.

Together, we will do great things.

Love,

Your Almost Wife

At her wedding reception, Maeve found a note tied with a white ribbon on her dinner plate. Her new husband was speaking to his out-of-town rela-tives as she opened it. She found a handwritten message on stationery engraved with her new mar-ried name, *Maeve MacDougal Black*.

   My Mouse-

I couldn't wait to see your name with mine, so I had this made for you. I hope you like it. I do (and I do and I do).

   Forever yours,
   Douglas

Your wedding day is rich with opportunities to give your love a letter or note. Think about it ahead of time, though, so your sentiment won't get lost in the shuffle, chaos, and jitters of that special day.

ANNIVERSARIES

Just as meaningful as your wedding day, anniversaries are obvious marks for love letters. You don't have to write one for every year, although an anniversary archive is a lovely idea. When the mood suits you or if you've had a particularly important or difficult year in your marriage, your anniversary can provide an occasion on which you can start over, adjust your emotional attitude, and feel refreshed in your relationship.

   Dear Angel,

I know this was a tough year, but we got through it. They say what doesn't kill you makes you stronger, so I guess we're both champions.

I know that the move was tough on you, and that my absence made things worse. I wish I could have been more attentive and that I was better at saying these things. I do love you, and I want you to know that I will try to make you happy—at least happier—this year.

Happy eighth anniversary.

Love,

Tony

BIRTHDAYS

Sometimes the best present you can give someone is your love in a letter. It's the kind of gift that doesn't cost much and is certainly very valuable. If you want to do it right, choose beautiful paper and the right kind of pen, and practice what you want to say before you write it down. Here's one that a friend of mine received on her fiftieth birthday at a time when she was feeling a little down.

My Own Bunny,

I am celebrating a great day today. It's your birthday, and a day that I know you've been dreading. Here's how I see it.

You're the woman whom I have always loved and will always love. You're my soul mate and the magic in my life, every day. I look around at our friends and the people I work with, and they don't have what we have.

There's not a woman in the world who can hold a candle to you. I mean it. So my Bunny, don't torture yourself with the number of years gone by. They were good years, and we have more to come.

I love you now and I'll love you all the way.

Your Fox

Don't forget that you can use humor, too. Your love letters need not only take on deep sentiment or heavy-going quotations. Here's a card written by a man who refused to give in to buying birthday greeting cards, even though he knew his wife liked to receive them (especially the funny kind).

Because I know that you like birthday cards,
I went to the store and read them all . . .
But all of this hellish garbage would have been an insult to the warmest, funniest, sexiest, and smartest wife I would ever have dreamed of.
Happiness and fun in your new year!

NEW BABY

Laura and John had three children, and with each new baby, Laura wrote a note to John. She wrote them with the intention that her children would read them later in their lives, so that they could gain perspective on their parents' lives at the time each child was born. Laura's idea proved very special. As her children became parents themselves, each received the letter Laura had written at his or her birth. Inspired, her children carry on the tradition.

Dear John,

Thank you for being such a loving husband. I know that this year was difficult, with buying the house and making ends meet, but having John Jr. seems to make all of those tense days disappear, as if they never happened. We have the beginning of our family now, and holding John Jr. brings sweet tears to my eyes, just the way those same tears came when I said "I do" to you only a year ago.

Thank you for giving me my son. I love you,
Laura

Dear John,

Even though you were in Chicago yesterday, when our little Melody decided to come earlier than we thought, I felt as if you were right by my side. She's a beautiful sight. She has blond hair just like you, and a squished little nose that I suppose will turn out just fine. I love her so much. And I know that John Jr. will love her too. My mother said he's doing just fine and asked when he could play with his new sister.

Again, you've made me so happy. Our family is growing just perfectly.

I miss you, darling.

Your Laura

Dear John,

I'm tired but so happy I can't sleep. Sally arrived like a cork popping out of a bottle. The doctor said she's very tiny but completely healthy, thank goodness.

I keep thinking of all the things I didn't finish in the new house—the curtains in the girls' room, mending John Jr.'s scout uniform—all the things that keep me so busy every day. I wish you wouldn't have to travel so much, but I am grateful that your work is going so well. I think of how lucky our children are to have a father so loving and strong. Sally comes into such a happy family.

The nurse just told me to stop writing and get some rest. I suppose she's right. I won't be sleeping much when I get home.

I love you, John. Even more than on our wedding day.

Laura

More Rites of Passage

Almost every occasion you experience in your family life will give you an opportunity to write a love letter. You don't have to seize every moment, though. Simply choose those times when you feel you want and need to express your affection. You can still keep flames of love alive even when other people (children, parents, relatives) seem to take over all of your time together.

MOVING

Today, people seem to move around more than they used to, for new jobs or better lifestyles, or just for new experiences. No matter how often you move, though, it's always a total upheaval of your lives and your habits. You have to resettle and, in a way, recommit to your lives together.

Writing a love letter during a move can anchor the feelings you have for each other, allaying some of the stress that comes with the territory. Even if your short temper gets the better of you, a love letter or at least a love note can keep the basic structure of your relationship healthy and remind you of just why you want to live together.

Dear Charlie,
I want you to know that our life together brings me more happiness and fulfillment than I ever thought possible. If you could just remember to put your dirty

clothes in the hamper in the new house, I will think I live in heaven.

I love you even though you're a slob.

Isabel 🐚

NEW JOBS AND PROMOTIONS

Your love life at some point will give way to your regular life or your working life. This is normal, but sometimes it is disappointing when we don't seem to live up to those fabulous, full-color moments we see in movies and read about in books. To keep the love pulsing through all parts of your life, try writing a love letter of congratulations. You can infuse your connection with a new-found pride and passion.

🐚 *Dear Coby,*

I knew from the moment you smiled at me that you would one day have the world in your hand. I'm so proud of you. I'm proud that you chose me to be your wife; I'm proud that you've been so loyal and trusting; I'm proud that you're so wonderful to the kids I brought into this marriage. But really, my darling, I'm bursting with pride on your new role as Vice President. No one deserves success more than you do.

You may address me as "Mrs. Vice President," if you please!

 Love,

 Marybeth

COMMUNIONS, CONFIRMATIONS, BAR OR BAT MITZVAHS

When these auspicious religious occasions arise for your children, you might find yourself caught up in their lives, their energy, their problems. Your "coupleness" has probably been lost for quite some time, since growing children can be brutal on passionate and romantic time together.

You don't have to let your kids' lives dampen your romantic spirit. You can keep things lively and intimate by exchanging a few love letters here and there.

 Dear Jean,

 Did you know that I got a tear in my eye watching Marie in her first Communion? I am so happy we have such a great family. Thank you for being a wonderful mother and thank you for making me so happy. It's in these odd moments that I remember how much I love you.

 Henry

GRADUATIONS

Graduations inspire deep emotions in couples. Your child's accomplishment is a source of pride as well as a grand marker of time. (How did she get to be so big?)

> *Darling Kerry,*
>
> *Our little Patootie is now a big-deal college graduate. Have you ever been so proud of her? We have a great daughter.*
>
> *And now she's off to her life without us. No tuition checks to pay, no last-minute laundry to do. What will we do with ourselves?*
>
> *I have an idea. Let's have a real date—the kind we had when we first met. Let's take a walk, get an ice cream, maybe kiss in the park. Then let's drink some champagne. I love you and after all, now I have time (and money!) to show it.*
>
> *Love,*
> *Keith*

FAMILY AFFAIRS

In families, things change with the wind. One day you're the daughter and, in what feels like a brief gust of wind, you're a grandmother. Every family event is a hallmark of love and provides an opportunity for a love letter. While you may think that love letters are for youngsters, they're not exclusive to any age. Writing gets better with age.

To My Loving New Grandma/Wife,

We've turned so many pages in our life together. So many firsts. When we first met, when we first made love, our first anniversary, and our first child. How can it be, that we are just now starting another new chapter? How did you make the time go so fast?

This is a glorious day. I love the idea that there is a new generation, carrying our name, and making our family just that much more complete. This will be a great adventure to share. You are destined to become the most wonderful (and, did I mention sexy?) grandmother of all time. I just hope I can keep up with you.

Thank you for turning my life into a glorious journey of love. Now, go shopping. There must be a dozen things you need in order to start properly spoiling her!

With love,
George

SAFE DEPOSIT BOX

You may not want to think about it, but one day all that will be left of you is what you leave behind. Sure, you have a will that will record your last wishes, but wouldn't it be wonderful if the love you feel for your family right this minute could be sealed in a time capsule? It can be.

Here's a letter that would make anyone grieving the loss of a father feel deeply comforted.

To My Darling Children,

Many cultures believe that a person never truly dies as long as he or she is remembered by others. Our family memory holds treasures far greater than anything you will find in this box of meager material possessions.

My "wealth" was never based on numbers listed in a checkbook, or in some IRA account. You, my family, provided me with everything a man could ever need. It all begins with the love your cherished mother shared with all of us.

She was that saving grace who touched my soul, inspired me to give love, and who led me to try to be the best father possible, even with all of my limitations and flaws. We should all thank her for being the rock on which the foundation of this family was built, and the glue that held us together. I will love her forever.

They say in heaven the love of God is greater than the love any one human being can have for another. I don't know how that's possible, since I love your mother so much. Still, if it is true, then we can all look forward to the day when we will be together, living with a love far greater than even the small glimpse we shared with each other on earth.

Don't grieve me. Celebrate us. And always remember the place you held in our hearts, as we grew old together, and as we rest eternally now.

 Love,
 Dad

Love Letters That Travel

Most of us lead lives punctuated with packed schedules and responsibilities, many times involving travel. If you find yourself constantly on the run and feeling out of touch with your mate, you can keep in touch with strategically placed notes of love.

For instance, Mick and Judy ran into a bad scheduling problem when he took a job in sales for his security company. Judy, a nurse, worked a shift starting at 7 A.M. and often took weekend overtime. She was up and out of the house before Mick woke up in the morning. They barely overlapped at home and at one point, they hadn't seen each other in more than two weeks. Judy started to slip little love notes into Mick's suits when they came back from the cleaners, just to keep him on his toes.

In a meeting one day, Mick reached into a pocket and pulled out a note that said, "Hi honey. I'm thinking of you right now and I miss you. Love, Judy."

On another trip, he found a note in his briefcase that said, "I love you and miss you. I hope when you find this you're on your way home."

Mick responded so warmly to her little notes that Judy bought special stationery. Mick started receiving scented notes, checklists for happiness, and even paper airplanes. Judy had such fun with the idea, and she continues to slip Mick notes today, even though he's home much more often.

You can do the same thing: slip notes into a pocket, a suitcase, or a coat. A spontaneous love note can put a little zing into your relationship without the need for a well-thought-out or special message. You can even express your friskier sentiments, but be sure to put these notes in a safe, personal place. You don't want the wrong person to read them.

One last thing: E-mail does not work well for this kind of gesture. There's one simple reason: it's too easy. The element of surprise is important for these little notes to be successful. It's one thing to find a message waiting for you on a computer screen and quite another to find it tucked into your toiletries bag. E-mail cheats your loved one of the dramatic effect a real note can have.

Recently, a friend took her daughter to her husband's office for Take Your Daughter to Work Day. While her husband went about showing their daughter around, my friend flipped through a pad of Post-its and wrote naughty, intimate messages throughout. Sure, it was a little risky, but days later, when her husband noticed them, he called her and laughed and thanked her for the joke. Love letters can bring a smile to your lover's face for a lot of different reasons!

Healing Letters of Love

APOLOGIES

When an apology is called for, you can more comfortably express in a letter what can be so hard to say out loud. Writing a letter gives you time to choose your words, experiment with your tone, and finally say exactly what you want in the most effective way possible.

While a love letter may not be right for saying "Sorry I spilled the milk," it can be a great form of healing for something like "Sorry I spilled the beans," or "Sorry I hurt your feelings."

You have to assume that you're going to do something at some point that will hurt your mate's feelings. You will then want to make amends, and candy, flowers, dinner, a gift are all nice offerings, but writing a heartfelt apology complete with love has the greatest chance of truly healing the rift.

Dear Meredith,

We've survived worse, I know, but for some reason this fight has hit me on a much deeper level. Why do we always fight when I have to leave town? Here I am on the plane headed toward Omaha and you're sitting back home where I want to be, if only to hug you and tell you that I'm so, so sorry that we fight.

Even though it's corny, I do feel as if you're my everything. I can't imagine not coming home to you, having anyone else be the mother of my children. I can't imagine a life without you. I love you so much that I'm even writing this letter to tell you.

I know I'll call you before you get this. I know our fight will probably already be long over. (I'm ready to give in.) Just know that my heart hurts when you're so angry with me and I guess I'm even a tiny bit afraid that you'll decide I'm just not worth putting up with.

Please don't get there.

Love,

Barney

HEALING WORDS FOR ILLNESS

When someone you love gets sick, it's tough on everyone. You'll worry, you might feel frightened; not everyone can face illness with a stiff upper lip.

It doesn't have to be a life-threatening illness to make you feel anxious, either. When anyone you love is in pain or discomfort, you want to be there with them to help them get better. It's a great time to write a love letter.

  Dear Rose,

I know you hate all of those tests they're giving you. Believe me, if I could take them for you, I would. I don't think the doctor is worried that there's anything seriously wrong, but I know you're scared. Let me tell you what I do know.

I know that you're a brilliant, brightly lit person. I know that you're pretty on the outside but really amazingly beautiful on the inside. I know that you have courage and softness at the same time, and that you have made me a very, very happy man.

I know that our kids have some of your light inside them, too. But most of all, I know that you're going to be just fine. You'll be home in no time and telling me to close the screen door and to please fix the toaster (no, I haven't done it yet).

I love you, my sweet Rose. Please don't let your heart feel heavy. I think you just ate a bum egg.

Love you forever,
Hopeton

JUST BECAUSE

Whatever your occasion may be, if you're moved to write a love letter, do it. You can put one in the glove compartment of a new car, or into a lunch bag or gym bag. The element of surprise and "no occasion at all" can make the message even more powerful than when it's expected. Use the rhythm of your relationship and commitment to your love life to inspire you to find the right time to write.

5

Continuing Inspiration and Creativity

How do I love thee?
Let me count the ways.
I love thee to the depth and
breadth and height
My soul can reach,
when feeling out of sight
For the ends of Being and ideal Grace.

—ELIZABETH BARRETT BROWNING,
"SONNETS FROM THE PORTUGUESE"

*O*nce you've entered into the habit of writing love letters, you might want to branch out into more creative areas or maybe push your "muse" into new places.

In Chapter One, you were encouraged to find your romantic voice through different sources of inspiration, such as music, art, poetry, or nature. Almost everything in life can inspire a love letter. All it really takes are your love and vision to make that connection. Now you can continue to explore your ability by using more sophisticated phrasings and descriptions.

Metaphors and Similes

You've probably already used metaphors and similes without realizing it. Just to refresh that high-school grammar, here's what we're talking about, according to the American Heritage Dictionary.

A metaphor is "a figure of speech in which a word or phrase that ordinarily designates one thing is used to designate another, thus making an implicit comparison, as in 'a sea of troubles.'"

A simile is "a figure of speech in which two essentially unlike things are compared, often in a phrase introduced by like or as, as in 'How like the winter hath my absence been' or 'So are you to my thoughts as food to life' (Shakespeare)."

Countless writers rely on metaphors and similes to describe feelings and add a dimension of illustration to their point. Just look at how a flat phrase can become more poetic and emotional.

- Flat phrase: You played the piano so well it took my breath away.
- Metaphor: Your music almost drowned me with its force and depth, in waves so powerful I surrendered myself without a fight.
- Simile: Your hands playing the piano are like an angel strumming lightly on a harp, producing music so heavenly I don't want to breathe and interrupt the pleasure.

In writing about love, similes and metaphors are practically unavoidable: "My love is like a crackling fire: hot, consuming, and a little dangerous."

Notice the similes employed in this love poem by John Clare, written in the nineteenth century.

FIRST LOVE

I ne'er was struck before that hour
With love so sudden and so sweet,
Her face it bloomed like a sweet flower

And stole my heart away complete,
My face turned pale as deadly pale,
My legs refused to walk away,
And when she looked, what could I ail?
My life and all seemed turned to clay.

And then my blood rushed to my face
And took my eyesight quite away,
The trees and bushes round the place
Seemed midnight at noonday.
I could not see a single thing,
Words from my eyes did start —

They spoke as chords do from the string,
And blood burnt round my heart.

Are flowers the winter's choice?
Is love's bed always snow?
She seemed to hear my silent voice,
Not love's appeals to know.
I never saw so sweet a face
As that I stood before,

My heart has left its dwelling-place
And can return no more.

Understandably, you might be a little shy about employing such obviously romantic tactics. You might be afraid of sounding corny or contrived. Don't do anything you don't feel comfortable with, but do experiment with the idea.

Dear James,

These long winter's nights seem to yawn with loneliness. You've only been gone for a few days but I miss your strong arms and warm breath on my back at night. You're like my security blanket, quietly there for me if I need you, soft and warm, full of comfort.

I know I'm a big girl now and I don't really need that blanket, but it sure feels good and—you know, I've loved you for a long time. I know you're away for three whole months and that you'll be back when spring is already here, but I want to clutch you to me any time of year.

I love you, my darling. Fuzzy bits and all.

Your Charlotte

To help you along, here are some ideas for expanding your use of metaphors. While they might sound corny or inappropriate to your relationship, they're here to give you ideas, to provoke your own creative juices to flow in new directions.

If you're weak on subject matter, here are some

areas you might like to try. You can always turn to country and western music, too, which makes use of no end of descriptive comparisons.

SAMPLES OF METAPHORS AND SIMILES

- Your hair falling against my face is like the gentle caress of a goddess.
- Your hair is a warm, golden blanket of bliss.
- Your small fingers are like jewels that beg to be held.
- I look into your eyes, a well of deep love, beauty, and soulful power.
- The angle of your cheek beckons kisses like the red flag entices the bull to charge.
- Your lips are like ripe fruit, glistening, waiting to be nibbled.
- Your sweet voice is like a song from heaven's angels and the devil's best sinner.
- Watching you walk away is a symphony of feminine fluttering and genius poise.
- Your wit cuts me like a knife, sharpened with passion and attitude.

Subjects for Comparisons

There are so many opportunities for comparison that it's impossible to list them all. However, to give you a push, here are some subjects that are easy to use.

Body parts: Hair, neck, face, eyes, brows, nose, lips, mouth, cheeks, arms, hands, fingertips, breasts, waist, legs

Nature: Flowers (roses, daisies, lilacs), sunshine, moonlight, blue sky, fields, pastures, mountains, oceans, lakes, rivers, streams

Arts: Music, art, poetry, dance, sculpture

Dear Lola,

I'm a silly poet and I know it, but I'm feeling up to sharing this one with you.

My love is like a gorgeous day,
With sun and wind so strong.
I whisk and run and want to play
With you the whole day long.

Continuing Inspiration and Creativity

But nighttime falls and we must go
Inside and get some rest.
And in the moonlight now I know
The dark with you is best.

If there's a line between sweet and terrible poetry,
I assume I'm standing on it.
Love,
Rudy

ROLE-PLAYING

If you feel like raising the stakes of your communications, try a little acting. It does wonders for your romantic life and can have positive side effects on your more intimate contact.

For instance, as a couple you probably have some favorite movies or common interests. These make great platforms for role-play in your love letters. Flora and Drew both like to read murder mysteries, and when Flora wanted to write a little lovey note to jostle Drew out of a difficult time at work, she resorted to role-playing.

Dear Detective Drew,

I would like to call to your attention a matter of grave importance. I seem to be missing my boyfriend. He was here only a few days ago, but I fear he has been

*taken over by an alien life force that keeps him at his
desk from early morning until very late at night. He
hasn't taken pleasure with me for at least a week.*

*I fear for his life, dear detective. Do you think you
could solve this very pressing case?*

With best regards,

Flora in Flux 🐚

Unlike Flora, Zoe needed something to give her husband for their anniversary but didn't have a lot of money to spend. Since her husband, Sam, had just been through an annoying car-inspection process, Zoe chose to use it as a way to bring a little light into their anniversary. For effect, she typed her note on her computer with a typeface that closely resembled that of a bureaucratic form letter.

🐚 *To Whom It May Concern:*

*You are due for a critical inspection and registration
updates for the new year. Kissing, hugging, and various
expressions of love will be tested at that time and critical
documents will be reviewed. Should you pass inspection,
your papers will be renewed for one year. Please make an
appointment for this tune-up by the thirteenth of the next
month.*

*Inspector of Passion and Romance for Marriage
Renewal Licenses* 🐚

You can take role-playing far in your love letters. I know couples who refer to each other by their respective roles both in letter writing and in public. It's a great form of intimate expression that can grow with your relationship and your years together.

Dear Doctor,

I am feeling rather low these days, and I was hoping you'd come for a house call. I understand that this is a great favor to ask, but I do believe I'm in danger.

Please visit me this evening, after 7 P.M. I have a sirloin that is in need of surgery and a cork in need of extraction.

Of course, I will reward you handsomely.

Your patient Patient

Enclosures

While it has been touched on briefly in previous chapters, the subject of enclosures is worth a closer look. Your love letters can be greatly enhanced with a little addition to your words.

An enclosure isn't a gift. It's more a token or form of intimacy or enticement. An enclosure is something that says you have a special connection no one else can share.

Here's an example of a letter that flirts and invites and uses an enclosed object to entice.

✎   *Dear Lydia,*

I understand this may come as some surprise to you, but I must confess I have an enormous appetite. As you can see by the matches I've enclosed, I know that this particular restaurant, Chez Pascal, is the only place that will satisfy my craving.

In addition to my urgent need to dine out, I must also enlist your help in another matter. You see, I hate to dine alone and the very thought of doing so leaves me incapable of swallowing (you see how this poses a serious threat to my health as well as being problematic in actually eating).

Here is where I hope you will be kind enough to join me for dinner. I have a certain picture in my head, or maybe it's better called a vision. I'll describe it to you.

A bottle of vintage champagne is in its bucket. Small candles are flickering on the table, and the most magnificent aroma of delicately roasting meats and vegetables is drifting from the kitchen. (Oh, my mouth is watering).

I sit comfortably in my chair and raise my glass — to you, sitting across from me, with your dark red hair framing your lovely brown eyes, which look back into mine. We don't even need to speak, for the moment's beauty is simple and quiet.

These matches hold the spark to light many flames, fires, and candles. If you would share an evening with me and make my vision become a reality, who knows how many sparks may ignite.

I do hope you'll agree to find out.

Guy 🖋

Matchbooks, Cracker Jack toys, even a blade of grass have been used as little enclosures to add power or mystery to a love letter. While you're in a flirtatious mode, keep anything you use light and easy. The letter Guy wrote to Lydia teetered on the edge of "too much"; his intention was to woo and not to come off sounding like a stalker or a nut. He was able to straddle romance and his own eccentric humor to make this letter palatable.

Here's another example of a playful letter, this time using the baseball season's schedule as a little enticement.

Dear Malcolm,

Have you seen the recent Cardinals schedule? If not, here it is.

I never had more fun at a game than when I ran into you at the stadium last summer. I'd sure love to do it again.

I have great seats for the July 15th home game and

I'm hoping you'll want to join me. I'll buy the peanuts
and Cracker Jacks. (I don't care if I never get back.)
　　Hope you'll go to first base!
　　Babs

When your relationship goes a little deeper, you
can get into more personal, romantic enclosures.
You might think this is for sissies, but it's not—
especially when you want to make a point. Of the
many elements you can use for enclosures, classics
include poems, pressed flowers, and locks of hair.
Scent, too, can add a particular dimension that is
romantic, intimate, and entirely individual.

　Dear Thomas,
　　You've always shown me the greatest attention and
respect, and for that I want to thank you. You've also
given me the most amazing and wonderful gift of your
love, which still makes my eyes a little misty.
　　I don't know how to show you how much I care for
you, too, because last night the words just didn't seem
to come so easily. I want you to know that I love you
very much—I just don't know how to say it or show it
very well.
　　When I was young, my father told me a story about
our family, and it's something I want to share with you.
　　My great-great-grandparents lived in different villages

when they were children, but they saw each other at the church festivals and sometimes in the market. Legend has it that they loved each other at first sight, but didn't know each other's names. To show how much she cared for him, my mother cut a little lock of hair off where no one would notice, and tied it with special ribbon. She carried it with her whenever she thought she might run into him, as one day she did. It was at the marketplace, and her mother told her to buy some bread. At the baker's table, she noticed him holding a basket for his own mother. She waited for him to catch her eye while his mother was busy picking out apples. She ran up to him, thrust the lock of her hair into his hand, and ran away.

My great-great-grandfather spent the next few years trying to see her again, but to no avail. He finally thought that her family had moved away and gave up hope. Just then he saw her in the market again, grown taller, even prettier. He himself had become a young man and, with a young man's courage, he ran up to my grandmother and showed her the hair he still carried.

They were allowed to marry and—well, I guess they lived happily ever after.

This story is a long and probably embellished way of telling you that I love you and that this small lock of hair enclosed is a way of showing you how deeply my feelings run.

Ever yours,

Krista

Dear Maxine,

You know that I can't write. But someone showed me this poem in a book of quotations and I thought of you.

Love,

Brandon

Give me a kiss, and to that kiss a score;
Then to that twenty, add a hundred more:
A thousand to that hundred: so kiss on,
To make that thousand up a million.
Treble that million, and when that is done,
Let's kiss afresh, as when we first begun.

—ROBERT HERRICK, 1591–1674,
"TO ANTHEA: AH, MY ANTHEA!"

A pressed flower or some petals are very romantic and can be symbolic of an occasion or event.

Dear Duane,

Our wedding day is still fresh in my mind although it was thirty-five years ago. I still love you as much as, if not more than, when we said our vows.

I pressed this flower the day of our wedding, just before I left for the church. I must have forgotten about it but in my spring cleaning spree I dusted the old dictionary and it popped out.

I take it as a sign that it's time to share it with you.

You are my great love, my only love, and I look to the future hoping for thirty-five more years with you.

Love,

Sheila

Grand Gestures in Writing

If you've had any success with your letter writing by now—and you must be successful by now—it's time to give one last push to a higher level of intensity.

You might have chosen a light and easy style for your love letters so far, but if you have a courageous heart and a willing pen, you are ready for the grand gesture. Just remember that grand gestures and big romantic statements should be used sparingly so that your efforts are taken seriously. You don't want to overwhelm the object of your affection; but you do want him or her to know that your feelings have reached a peak you want to share.

Here are some grand statements that might help you come into your own way of saying things.

- *You're like a luminous being, lighting up a room with a mere hint of your presence.*
- *Your eyes could tantalize a lobster into a pot of boiling-hot water. Just imagine what they do to me!*

- *Your eyes pierce through the fog of my confusion, cutting a clear path into my heart.*
- *They say the eyes are the windows of the soul. Yours are so much more. They are my redemption.*
- *A kiss from you is sweeter, richer, and more satisfying than a Mississippi Mud Pie.*
- *When we kiss, the heavens stop so the angels can see the closest thing to a perfect love upon the earth.*
- *A kiss from you is the whipped cream and cherry on this sundae called life.*
- *Our love is a garden. With the right light and care, we can produce great bounty.*
- *Your wit slices through my awkward silences and reduces me to such great laughter.*
- *Holding your hand is like walking with my greatest dream come true.*
- *Style is the word invented to describe you. Kissing you melts my heart.*
- *When I kiss you, each and every time I am amazed by the sheer softness of your lips.*
- *When we kiss I am complete. It takes no more than the gentle touch of your lips against mine.*
- *Being with you inspires me to heights I never thought I would see or visit. You give me the will to be more than I am.*
- *Your love is the rock. It is the foundation on which the rest of my life is built.*

- *Our love soars higher than the heights of the tallest mountain.*
- *Our time together suspends eternity as we live forever in a single moment.*
- *Before you, life was an empty vessel. After you, my cup is full.*
- *Holding you is hanging on to every morsel of meaning that life can render.*
- *Your touch is my absolution.*
- *Your voice is the cherished song of morning lark, singing of love, life, and the freedom to live.*

Your Own Fairy Tale

This may be going too far for some of you, but there is nothing more romantic than writing your own fairy tale complete with happy ending. Since it's yours, you can incorporate anyone who plays an important role in your life.

Final Words

*N*ow we have escorted you through the process of writing a love letter. It's time for you to write one on your own.

You can do it! You know you can. You must take a chance at least once in your life to explore your feelings on paper.

You may think you've already done so — remember the letter you wrote to your first crush in seventh grade? Maybe your youth propelled you into writing, and all of your growing vocabulary (not to mention hormones) helped you along. Today, though, you're a different person; in ten years you'll be different again. Your writing will go through changes. It will mature; your style might become more minimalist or more florid, and you might be influenced by fads. (If you're a fan of William Safire, however, you'll be current with the fashions and why they're not good for language). At any rate, your personality and life evolve with the years, and so do your voice and, of course, your love.

Ideally, your love will expand as you grow older, but it's just possible that it will become complacent. The youthful vigor of age fourteen can peak on a wedding day and then just peter out, collapsing with the comfort of a secure marriage or relationship.

Yet, this is precisely the time when you need to be writing to your love—about your love—even more. Love letters keep you fresh, interesting, passionate, and, one hopes, honest about your feelings.

Writing a love letter can be a meditation, in a way. The process compels you to feel, to describe what you feel, and to purposefully address your feelings to your loved one. Even if you don't send the letter, you have done something honorable: you've consciously recognized your emotional self, and the integrity of that act cannot be disputed.

Avoid emotional complacency if you can. Although the theory is not medically proven, you'll probably live a longer, happier life if you continue to evolve emotionally.

Write for yourself, not for someone else. The worst mistake you can make in a love letter is to say what you think the other person wants you to say rather than what you really want to say.

Men, remember: don't try to win points by writing phony love letters with hearts, rainbows, flowers, and butterflies (or whatever you *think* a woman will like). Women might think it's cute at first, but if you can't live up to a tender thought, it's not believable and you'll come off badly.

Ladies: on the other hand, do not indulge yourself too much with description, verbiage, or humor, and *never* apologize for what you want to say. Stop if you find yourself writing like this:

- "I'm not really a good writer but I just want you to know that . . ."
- "I'm really bad at this sort of thing, but . . ."
- "This might sound stupid, but . . ."

Got it? Any apology for your style, however sweet and timid it might be, doesn't do justice to your message. Anyone who loves you will honor your words, whatever they are. That's just what love is about.

If you happen to save letters written to you by people who are no longer in your life, do not dishonor them by laughing at them with others. You

wouldn't want that to happen to your letters and —
really — if you thought they were stupid or silly you
wouldn't have saved them, would you?

So get your thoughts and feelings ready to be
written down. We live in an age of hyper-
communication. Shouldn't a good portion of all of
these messages be about love?

If you need another nudge to get going, consider this scenario. You're on your deathbed. You
can sum up your life with one of these phrases: I
was really cool or I was well loved.

Which one is you? Get writing, and you can be
both.

Index

Index

About the Authors

BARRIE DOLNICK is the author of the very successful Simple Spells books. She is also a high-profile consultant whose company, Executive Mystic, uses alternative information techniques—tarot cards, astrology, meditation, and spell casting—to guide clients to fulfill their potential. She lives in New York City.

DONALD BAACK, Ph.D., is a professor of management at Pittsburg State University in Kansas. He lives near Carl Junction, Missouri.